Unity in Action

Unity in Action

by
John MacArthur, Jr.

MOODY PRESS
CHICAGO

All Scripture quotations, unless noted otherwise, are from the *New Scofield
Reference Bible*, King James Version. Copyright © 1967 by Oxford Univer-
sity Press, Inc. Reprinted by permission.

Library of Congress Cataloging in Publication Data

MacArthur, John F.
  Unity in action.

(John MacArthur's Bible studies)
Includes indexes.
  1. Christian life—1960-   2. Fellowship—
Religious aspects—Christianity.   I. Title.
II. Series: MacArthur, John F.   Bible studies.
BV4501.2.M163   1987   248.4   87-17176
ISBN 0-8024-5307-4

1 2 3 4 5 6 7 Printing/LC/Year 91 90 89 88 87

Printed in the United States of America

Contents

These Bible studies are taken from messages delivered by Pastor-Teacher John MacArthur, Jr., at Grace Community Church in Panorama City, California. The recorded messages themselves may be purchased as a series or individually. Please request the current price list by writing to:

WORD OF GRACE COMMUNICATIONS
P.O. Box 4000
Panorama City, CA 91412

Or call the following toll-free number:
1-800-55-GRACE

1
Receiving One Another with Understanding—Part 1

Outline

Introduction
A. The Danger of Sin
   1. The instruction of Christ
   2. The instruction of Paul
      a) In 1 Corinthians
      b) In 2 Corinthians
      c) In 2 Thessalonians
      d) In Romans
B. The Danger of Discord
   1. The issue
      a) Ephesians 4:3
      b) Colossians 3:14
      c) John 13:35
   2. The illustrations
      a) Acts 20:35
      b) Galatians 6:1
      c) 1 Thessalonians 5:14
   3. The implications
      a) Between strong and weak
         (1) The definitions
            (*a*) The strong
            (*b*) The weak
         (2) The temptation
            (*a*) The contempt of the strong
            (*b*) The condemnation of the weak
      b) Between Jew and Gentile
         (1) Christians from a Jewish background
         (2) Christians from a pagan background

Lesson

I. The Reception (v.17)
   A. The Conflict
      1. Identified
         a) Kosher Jews
         b) Pagan Gentiles
      2. Illustrated
         a) In Galatians 2
            (1) The confrontation
            (2) The cause
            (3) The cessation
               (a) Of the dietary laws
               (b) Of the Sabbath
            (4) The confusion
            (5) The correction
         b) In 1 Corinthians 8
            (1) A synopsis of the problem
            (2) A summary of the principles
               (a) Love must prevail
               (b) Idols are nothing
               (c) Food is not important
               (d) Liberty must not offend
   B. The Command
      1. The sacrifice of the strong
      2. The submission of the strong

Introduction

A. The Danger of Sin

Most Christians are aware of how sin can devastate a church. Sin can cripple the church's function, destroy its harmony, sap its strength, and negate its testimony. The New Testament calls for the purity of the church.

1. The instruction of Christ

In Matthew 18:15-17 Jesus instructs believers about how to deal with the sin of a fellow believer. First, He said, go and tell him of his sin. If he doesn't listen, bring witnesses. If he doesn't listen to the witnesses, tell the church. If he doesn't listen to the church, consider him

8

as you would an unbeliever. That passage is necessary because sin cripples believers.

2. The instruction of Paul

   a) In 1 Corinthians

   (1) The apostle Paul reminded the church at Corinth that "a little leaven leaveneth the whole lump" (5:6). The smallest sinful influence will have a pervasive effect in the church, just as yeast in a loaf of bread.

   (2) Before coming to the Lord's Table a man should "examine himself" to see if there is sin in his life (11:28).

   b) In 2 Corinthians

   Paul said, "Let us cleanse ourselves from all filthiness of the flesh and spirit, perfecting holiness in the fear of God" (7:1).

   c) In 2 Thessalonians

   Paul said to "withdraw yourselves from every brother that walketh disorderly" (3:6).

   d) In Romans

   In Romans there are many injunctions for the purity of the church. They begin in chapter 12, after Paul delineates the meaning of justification by grace through faith in the preceding chapters.

   (1) Our relationship to God

   Romans 12:1-2 says, "Present your bodies a living sacrifice, holy, acceptable unto God, which is your reasonable service. And be not conformed to this world, but be ye transformed by the renewing of your mind."

(2) Our relationship to the members of the Body of Christ (12:3-8).

(3) Our relationship to everyone

Paul said we are to show love, kindness, under-standing, and affection toward everyone (12:9-10). We should rejoice in hope and pray diligently for everyone (v. 12). We should give to people in need (v. 13). Verse 14 says, "Bless them who persecute you." Verse 20 says to feed your enemies. Verse 21 says, "Be not overcome by evil, but overcome evil with good."

(4) Our relationship to the government

We are to have an exemplary relationship to the government, which means submitting to authorities and paying our taxes (13:1-7).

(5) Our relationship to our neighbors

Romans 13:10 says, "Love worketh no ill to its neighbor." We are to owe no debt except the debt of love (v. 8).

Paul closes chapter 13 by urging believers to live a pure life. We should take stock of where we are and change our life-style if we need to by casting off the works of darkness and putting on the armor of light (v. 12). Verse 13 says, "Let us walk honestly, as in the day; not in reveling and drunkenness, not in immorality and wantonness, not in strife and envying." Romans 12-13 is a call for purity in the church. Righteousness, not sin, is the proper response to justification by grace through faith. Verse 14 concludes, "Put ye on the Lord Jesus Christ, and make not provision for the flesh, to fulfill its lusts."

The church must be pure. That's why there is a need for church discipline. We're to confess our sins to one another (James 5:16). We read the Word of God that sin might be exposed. We pray that the Spirit of God might reveal to us anything in our lives that isn't right. We're to offer reproof, instruction, guidance, and wisdom to one another to assist in the spiritual growth and purity of the church.

B. The Danger of Discord

However, sin is not the only problem the church faces. All churches have the potential for conflict between strong and weak believers. Although this is not strictly a sin problem, it can result in sin. In Romans 14:1–15:13 Paul discusses the unity of believers.

A Melting Pot of Diversity

Within the church, people are at different levels, both physically and spiritually. Some people have been saved fifty years; others have been saved less than a year. Some come from irreligious, atheistic, or humanistic backgrounds. Some used to be Mormons or Jehovah's Witnesses. Some come from legalistic fundamentalist churches; others come from loose, free-wheeling churches.

Diversity is often good, but it tends to bring about clashes. The church is made up of Christians at every level, but we all have one thing in common: although we have been redeemed, we are hindered by our flesh (Rom. 6-7). It is as important to deal with the conflict of diverse people, all with unredeemed flesh, as it is to deal with overt sin. Some people have asked me, "Why don't the women in your church wear hats?" They are concerned because they come from a background where women wore hats. Others have asked, "Why don't you use candles?" It is difficult for them to worship without candles because that has been their previous experience. Some have been offended by certain hairstyles. Some are offended by certain styles of music. Although some don't have a problem with drinking alcohol, others view it as a vile sin. Some go to movies, and others don't.

Within the church today new Christians are holding onto old habits and traditions. It takes time before they can let go of such things because they're so ingrained. People have preferences in everything from dress to music to diet to entertainment. That was true in the early church, and it is even more true in the American church because we are a melting pot of diversity.

Preferences aren't necessarily a sin issue, but they can become serious when people in the church can't get along with each other. So in Romans 14:1–15:13 Paul talks about the importance of unity.

1. The issue

   It is essential to maintain unity in the church.

   a) Ephesians 4:3—Paul said the church is to be "endeavoring to keep the unity of the Spirit in the bond of peace."

   b) Colossians 3:14—Paul said, "Above all . . . put on love, which is the bond of perfectness."

   c) John 13:35—The Lord said, "By this shall all men know that ye are my disciples, if ye have love one to another." Jesus prayed that we would be one, not only in our redemption but also in demonstrating that redemption to the world by our love for one another (John 17:21). However, this love comes with difficulty.

2. The illustrations

   a) Acts 20:35—Paul said to the elders at the church at Ephesus, "I have shown you all things, how that so laboring ye ought to support the weak." It is the strong who are to be conscientious about helping the weak.

   b) Galatians 6:1—Paul said, "Brethren, if a man be overtaken in a fault [the weak believer], ye who are spiritual [the strong believer] restore such an one in the spirit of meekness."

   c) 1 Thessalonians 5:14—Paul said, "We exhort you, brethren, warn them that are unruly." The "unruly" lack caution regarding their freedoms in Christ. They tend to be undisciplined, which is why they need to be warned. Paul then said, "Encourage the fainthearted." The "fainthearted" are those who are fearful of exercising their liberty. Paul concluded by saying, "Support the weak, be patient toward all men."

First John 2:13 tells us about infants, young men, and fathers in the faith, all on a continuum of spiritual growth. If we're to love each other as we should, we need to understand Paul's instruction in Romans 14:1–15:13.

3. The implications

   a) Between strong and weak

   (1) The definitions

   (*a*) The strong

   Liberated believers understand what it means to be free in Christ. They don't cling to meaningless traditions and forms of religion. They understand that they are free from sin, death, hell, and Satan. They understand that they are not obligated to follow holy days and ceremonies. They know they are free to make choices dependent on how the Spirit of God moves in their hearts. Such people are strong in the faith.

   (*b*) The weak

   The weak believers continue to hang onto the rituals and ceremonies of their past, refusing to let go. They don't believe they have freedom in Christ to do otherwise. Such freedom threatens them, so they prefer to remain as they are.

   (2) The temptation

   (*a*) The contempt of the strong

   The strong tend to look down on the weak as a legalistic, faithless people who get in the way of those who are trying to enjoy their liberty. They resent the weak for labeling their rightful freedoms in Christ as sin.

(b) The condemnation of the weak

The weak tend to condemn the strong for what they see as an abuse of liberty. However, they are not in the position to judge since they don't understand Christian liberty.

b) Between Jew and Gentile

As Christians we are free from the penalty of sin, the power of death, the punishment of hell, and the persuasion of Satan. We are free to worship and adore God. We are forgiven and will go to heaven. But there is another dimension to our freedom in Christ in the New Covenant: we are free from all the Old Testament ceremonial laws. We are not free from the Ten Commandments or any other moral law given in the Old Testament, but we are free from the external ceremonial rules and rituals, for they were attached only to a period of time and to the people of Israel.

The church at Rome was made up of two groups of believers.

(1) Christians from a Jewish background

Some Jewish Christians still adhere to the traditions in which they were raised. That was even a bigger problem in Paul's day. Many Jews who had been saved out of Judaism found it next to impossible to let go of their ingrained traditions, such as the observation of dietary laws, feast days, new moons, and Sabbaths. Throughout their lives they were expected to take part in those rituals. Acts 21:20 implies that most Jewish believers were still bound to the law of Moses. Their consciences put unnecessary bonds on their liberty in Christ.

14

(2) Christians from a pagan background

Other Christians in the church at Rome had been saved out of pagan idolatry. Like many of the Jewish Christians, they too were limited in their Christian freedom because of their former pagan practices. Many Gentiles were excusing themselves from eating certain foods that may have been offered to idols. Those foods were too much a part of their past for them to enjoy.

There were also mature, liberated believers in the church at Rome—both Jews and Gentiles—who were not bound in conscience by any of those things. They did not keep the Sabbath or observe the dietary laws, and they ate and drank whatever they wanted without regard for either Jewish law or pagan religion. The liberated believers saw the legalistic believers as sinfully bound to rules and traditions and despised their unbelief. On the other hand, the legalistic believers saw the liberated believers as sinful and condemned their liberty.

The conflict in the church at Rome was between the legalistic believer, who saw liberty as sinful, and the liberated believer, who saw legalism as sinful. Paul gave four principles to deal with that conflict: receiving one another with understanding (Rom. 14:1-12), building up one another without offending (14:13-23), pleasing one another for the sake of Christ (15:1-7), and rejoicing with one another in the plan of God (15:7-13).

Lesson

I. THE RECEPTION (v. 1)

"Him that is weak in the faith receive ye, but not to doubtful disputations."

15

A. The Conflict

1. Identified

   a) Kosher Jews

   The Jews had been raised to do what was kosher, which comes from the Hebrew word *kashar*, meaning "fit" or "right." The primary focus of *kashar* is on diet and the observation of special days. Leviticus 11 and Deuteronomy 14 detail the dietary restrictions. When Daniel was taken into captivity in Babylon he was told to eat the king's food, which wasn't kosher (Dan. 1:5). Verse 8 says Daniel decided not to eat it. He and his three friends—Hananiah, Azariah, and Mishael—would not compromise their Jewish convictions. Their actions were right, because God had ordained the dietary laws and those laws were still valid at that point in history.

   b) Pagan Gentiles

   The Gentile believers used to attend pagan festivals. Pagan festivals were basically drunken, gluttonous orgies. Their past experience with paganism drove many new Gentile converts away from things they were free to do as Christians.

2. Illustrated

   a) In Galatians 2

      (1) The confrontation

      Verse 11 says, "When Peter was come to Antioch, I [Paul] withstood him to the face, because he was to be blamed." Paul needed to confront Peter because Peter was a significant person in the Christian realm. He was an apostle of Christ in a way that Paul had not experienced. Peter lived and walked with Jesus Christ during His earthly ministry. Yet Peter did something that brought about a rebuke from Paul.

(2) The cause

Verse 12 says, "Before certain men came from James [the brother of the Lord and the leader of the church in Jerusalem], he [Peter] did eat with the Gentiles; but when they were come, he withdrew and separated himself, fearing them who were of the circumcision." Peter was afraid of what the Jewish visitors would think. That led him to deny the liberty he had in Christ by not sharing in a meal with the Gentile converts.

(3) The cessation

(*a*) Of the dietary laws

The Jewish dietary laws had been set aside in Acts 10:9-12. The Lord sent a vision to Paul of a sheet from heaven containing animals that were both clean and unclean—those that could be eaten and those that couldn't. The Lord told Peter, "Rise, Peter; kill, and eat" (v. 13). Peter said, "Not so, Lord; for I have never eaten anything that is common or unclean" (v. 14). The Lord replied, "What God hath cleansed, that call not thou common" (v. 15). The Lord eliminated all dietary restrictions.

(*b*) Of the Sabbath

The Lord eliminated the significance of the Sabbath when He said, "The Son of man is Lord even of the sabbath day" (Matt. 12:8). As far as the Jewish leaders were concerned, Jesus overtly violated the Sabbath and broke tradition. He rose from the dead on the first day of the week and established a new era in which the Sabbath no longer had significance. Peter was aware of that because he had been with Christ, saw Him after the resurrection, and knew the church initially met on the first day of the week (John 20:19).

(4) The confusion

When the Jews arrived from Jerusalem, Peter placed himself back under Mosaic law. Paul rebuked Peter for retreating from his liberty in Christ. He knew Peter's actions would bring confusion. Galatians 2:13 says, "The other Jews dissembled in like manner with him insomuch that Barnabas also was carried away with their hypocrisy." Peter's influential leadership caused the other Jews to withdraw from the Gentiles, and Paul could foresee a fracturing of the church.

(5) The correction

In Galatians 2:14 Paul says, "When I saw that they walked not uprightly according to the truth of the gospel, I said unto Peter before them all, If thou, being a Jew, livest after the manner of Gentiles, and not as do the Jews, why compellest thou the Gentiles to live as do the Jews?" Peter was wrong. That so great a leader as Peter could be misled illustrates the tremendous pressure for the early church to hang onto Judaism.

Acts 15:1-35 details the events surrounding the Jerusalem Council. Some of the church leaders wanted to hold to Judaism, especially a group known as Judaizers, who claimed a person couldn't be a Christian unless he kept the Mosaic law and was circumcised. Josephus, a first-century Jewish historian, said that some of the Jews at Rome ate only fruit for fear of eating something unclean (cited by Charles Hodge in *Commentary on the Epistle to the Romans* [Grand Rapids, Mich.: Eerdmans, 1977 reprint], p. 417). But the dietary laws had been abrogated long before. Jesus said, "There is nothing from outside of a man that, entering into him, can defile him; but the things which come out of him" (Mark 7:15). The pressure was on the Jews to maintain their heritage, and understandably they clung to it.

b) In 1 Corinthians 8

First Corinthians 8 gives insight into tensions Gentiles experienced in the early church and sheds light on tensions in the church today.

(1) A synopsis of the problem

Verse 1 begins, "Now as touching things offered to idols." Here is a synopsis of the problem in Corinth: a typical pagan worshiper would go to the temple of a pagan deity or to a festival and bring a sacrifice. He would offer vegetables, fruit, meat, or drink at the altar. A portion would be consumed in a ceremony, part would be eaten as a meal, and whatever was left would be sold in the market the next day. Anyone shopping at a temple market would purchase food that had been offered to idols.

A pagan who had been transformed by the gospel of Jesus Christ was understandably ashamed of his past involvement in idolatry. Being served food that had been offered to an idol would bother him greatly. Not eating that meal would offend the host, especially if he was a Jew who wasn't bothered by idols. But on the other hand, a Gentile host could offend a Jewish guest by offering him pork or any other animal that wasn't kosher.

(2) A summary of the principles

The problem within the Corinthian church was what to do with meat offered to idols. So Paul gave them some principles to guide their decisions.

(*a*) Love must prevail

First Corinthians 8:1-3 says, "Knowledge puffeth up, but love edifieth. And if any man think that he knoweth anything, he knoweth nothing yet as he ought to know. But if any man love God, the same is known of him." Paul was saying, "Don't force your knowledge on a person; rather, force your love on him." If you will offend a fellow believer by doing something, then don't do it. Be sensitive. Knowledge is fine, but love should prevail.

(b) Idols are nothing

Is there actually such a thing as a false god? No. So whatever is offered to a false god is offered to nothing. Verse 4 says, "As concerning, therefore, the eating of those things that are offered in sacrifice unto idols, we know that an idol is nothing in the world, and that there is no other God but one." There is no reason to be concerned about something offered to nothing, but that was hard for many to understand. Verses 5-6 say, "Though there be that are called gods, whether in heaven or in earth (as there are gods many, and lords many), but to us there is but one God, the Father, of whom are all things, and we in him; and one Lord Jesus Christ, by whom are all things, and we by him."

Verse 7 gives a different perspective: "However, there is not in every man that knowledge; for some with conscience of the idol unto this hour eat it as a thing offered unto an idol, and their conscience, being weak, is defiled." If the weaker brother eats meat sacrificed to idols without understanding why he can, he will defile his conscience, which tells him not to eat it. A man's conscience is controlled by his mind. It does not act independently of what he knows; it is simply set in motion by his mind. Thus when a weaker brother was convinced in his mind that the meat before him had been offered to a real idol yet he ate it anyway, his conscience reacted negatively to what he knew about that

20

meat. That's why Paul said not everyone knows that an idol is nothing (v. 7).

(c) Food is not important

Verse 8 says, "Food commendeth us not to God." God couldn't care less about what you eat in terms of its religious impact. God would not want you to eat something that would shorten your life or your ability to function, but God is not concerned with the kind of food you eat. Some people think vegetarians are spiritual and meat-eaters are not, but that's not true. Verse 8 continues, "For neither, if we eat, are we the better; neither, if we eat not, are we the worse." Paul says that eating meat offered to idols won't make you any better or any worse.

(d) Liberty must not offend

Verse 9 says, "Take heed lest by any means this liberty of yours becomes a stumbling block to them that are weak." If your liberty offends someone, don't exercise it. The people in the Corinthian church needed to hear that because some, having been saved out of paganism years before, were now buying their meat at the temple butcher shop. In turn they would invite new converts for dinner and offer them meat that had been offered to a false god. The new converts couldn't eat the meat without thinking they were worshiping a false god. The liberated believer would then try to convince the weak believer that he was free in Christ to eat whatever he wanted. But verse 11 says, "Through thy knowledge shall the weak brother perish, for whom Christ died?" Would you want to devastate someone for whom Christ died? Verse 12 says, "But when ye sin so against the brethren, and wound their weak conscience, ye sin against Christ." Paul concluded, "Wherefore, if food make my brother to offend, I will eat no meat

21

while the world standeth, lest I make my brother to offend" (v. 13).

From those two passages we see that many Jewish
believers were obsessed with maintaining Jewish traditions, and many Gentile believers were obsessed
with breaking away from pagan traditions. The potential for conflict in the church existed over those
issues.

B. The Command

Romans 14:1 refers to "him that is weak in the faith." The
present participle is used, indicating one who is being
weak in the faith. It is a failure of faith at a given moment or
circumstance, not necessarily a permanent state. The arti-
cle is present: he is weak in *the* faith. He is not weak in saving faith but in the faith necessary to believe he is free to
enjoy any kind of food or day and that he has cut off any
connection with the past.

1. The sacrifice of the strong

Paul told the strong to *receive* the weak in faith. The
Greek word translated "receive" means "to take to one-
self" and is preceded by the preposition *pros,* which in-
tensifies its meaning. Paul commanded the strong to
embrace the weak into their love and fellowship. Those
with a clear understanding of Christian freedom should
reach out and receive those with a lesser understanding.

A Day with the Amish

My wife, Patricia, and I visited Lancaster, Pennsylvania, years ago.
Among the people who live in the Lancaster area are the Amish.
The Amish live by a different set of standards than most of us.
Many of them own beautiful, prosperous farms. But they believe it
is sinful to travel by any vehicle powered by a motor.

We visited many Amish farms because Patricia was looking for
quilts, for which the Amish are known. As we visited one farm after another, we noticed that there were no televisions, radios, elec-

trical appliances, or automobiles. But curiously we often saw an engine-powered harvesting machine being pulled by horses!

At one Amish farm, we met a man who showed us his car, which he kept hidden in his barn. He also owned a radio. Somewhat sheepishly he said to me, "I'd like to ask you some Bible questions. I've been listening to you on the radio, and I really appreciate what you teach." It was obvious that he had come to know Christ. This man was fighting his liberation in Christ. He was starting to let go of some things while still holding onto others. He was letting it be known that he had a radio, and I think he had driven his car in the daytime. He wanted to know all about the book of Revelation because the Amish never interpret it. Patricia and I sat in the kitchen and answered question after question about the book of Revelation and the second coming of Christ. As we talked, I could see it was going to be difficult for this man to ever fully understand the freedom he could enjoy in Jesus Christ. If someone were to play Christian rock music for him or make him buy a three-piece pin-striped suit, he would be devastated.

There are many Christians who can't enjoy full liberty in Christ. We must love them and not do anything to offend them. That's what Paul is saying in Romans 14:1. If there is to be loving unity among believers, it must begin with the strong. The strong must be willing to sacrifice their liberties. Personally, I rejoice in doing so, because I want to do all I can for the sake of those who might be offended by my liberty. I want to receive them fully into the fellowship. So be sensitive to those who believe people ought to live a certain way, dress a certain way, and restrain from certain behavior. Wait until they can grow to understand their emancipation in Jesus Christ.

Paul's Harsh Words

Paul was gentle in his approach to the Romans on the subject of Christian liberty, but he strongly rebuked the Galatians and Colossians.

1. To the Galatians

In Galatians 1:8-9 Paul says, "Though we, or an angel from heaven, preach any other gospel unto you than that which we have preached unto you, let him be accursed. As we said before, so say I now again, If any man preach any other gospel unto you than that ye have received, let him be accursed." Paul is pronouncing a curse on anyone who preaches another gospel. The issue Paul is addressing is a distortion of the message of redemption. In Galatians 4:8-9 he says, "Nevertheless then, when ye knew not God, ye did service unto them which by nature are no gods. But now, after ye have known God, or rather are known by God, how turn ye again to the weak and beggarly elements, unto which ye desire again to be in bondage?"

After Paul preached the gospel in Galatia, Judaizers followed and said that grace can't save a person, claiming that true salvation must be accompanied by circumcision and obedience to the Mosaic law. In verses 10-11 Paul adds, "Ye observe days, and months, and times, and years. I am afraid of you, lest I have bestowed upon you labor in vain." In Galatians 5:1 he concludes, "Stand fast, therefore, in the liberty with which Christ hath made us free, and be not entangled again with the yoke of bondage." In verses 3-4 he says, "I testify again to every man that is circumcised. . . . Christ is become of no effect unto you."

Why was Paul so bold in his approach? Because the Judaizers were teaching the Galatian church that Mosaic law and ceremony were necessary for salvation. Paul condemned that as another gospel. However, the Roman church was not advocating those things as part of salvation—they believed in salvation by grace through faith in Christ alone.

2. To the Colossians

In Colossians 2:16-17 Paul says, "Let no man, therefore, judge you in food, or in drink, in respect of a feast day, or of the new moon, or of a sabbath day, which are a shadow of things to come; but the body is of Christ." Why did Paul tell the people to avoid those things? Because people were saying that to be a true Christian all those things had to be observed. They advocated those things as elements of salvation. Paul defiantly rejected that. But in the Roman church those things were not being claimed as necessary elements of salvation; they were merely vestiges of their past religion and thought necessary for spiritual growth.

2. The submission of the strong

In Romans 14:1 Paul says to receive the weak, "but not to doubtful disputations." The strong should not receive the weak to pass judgment on their opinions and argue with them. The purpose in receiving weaker believers is to love them.

Focusing on the Facts

1. What can sin do to a church (see p. 8)?
2. What instruction does Christ give for dealing with sin in the church (Matt. 18:15-17; see pp. 8-9)?
3. What are some of the injunctions Paul gives in Romans for the purity of the church (see pp. 9-10)?
4. What is another serious problem the church faces in addition to sin? Explain (see p. 11).
5. How do you define a strong believer (see p. 13)?
6. How do you define a weak believer (see p. 13)?
7. How are each of those believers tempted (see pp. 13-14)?
8. As Christians, from what are we free (see p. 14)?
9. Describe the kinds of people who existed in the church at Rome. In what ways did their backgrounds limit them (see pp. 14-15)?
10. What four principles does Paul give in Romans 14:1–15:13 for dealing with the conflict between weak and strong believers (see p. 15)?
11. Describe the confrontation that takes place in Galatians 2:11. Why does it occur (see pp. 16-17)?
12. Where in Scripture do we read that it is no longer necessary to observe the Jewish dietary laws and the Sabbath (see p. 17)?
13. What does the incident in Galatians 2:11-14 indicate about the pressure that existed for the Jewish Christian (see p. 18)?
14. Summarize the problem existing in Corinth with regard to strong and weak believers (see p. 19).
15. What principles did Paul present to the Corinthians for dealing with the problem of meat offered to idols? Explain (see pp. 19-21).

16. Explain how a man's conscience is controlled by his mind (see pp. 20-21).
17. According to Romans 14:1, what does Paul command the strong to do? Explain (see p. 22).
18. Why was Paul gentle to the Romans but harsh with the Galatians and Colossians over the issue of Christian liberty (see pp. 23-24)?

Pondering the Principles

1. Romans 12-13 discuss the believer's relationships with God and man. Review that section on pages 9-10. How would you best characterize your relationship with God, other believers, your neighbors, the government, and all people? Analyze each relationship. Slowly read Romans 12-13. What are the areas that need the greatest improvement? Commit yourself to making changes in those areas beginning this week. Remember, your commitment to be obedient in those areas affects the purity of the entire Body of Christ.

2. In Romans 14:1 Paul implores strong Christians to receive those who are weak in the faith. What is your level of commitment toward a Christian who has little understanding of his liberties in Christ? Are you making sacrifices of your liberties on his behalf? To help keep your responsibilities in mind, memorize 1 Corinthians 8:9: "Take care lest this liberty of yours somehow become a stumbling block to the weak" (NASB*).

*New American Standard Bible.

2
Receiving One Another
with Understanding—Part 2

Outline

Introduction

Review
I. The Reception (v. 1)

Lesson
II. The Reasons (vv. 2-12)
    A. The Lord Receives All Believers (vv. 2-3)
        1. Paul's generic description (v. 2)
            a) Of the strong
                (1) 1 Timothy 4:4-5
                (2) Acts 10:15
            b) Of the weak
                (1) Abstinence from vegetables
                (2) Abstinence from drink
        2. Paul's specific injunction (v. 3)
            a) The restriction (v. 3*a-b*)
                (1) For the strong (v. 3*a*)
                (2) For the weak (v. 3*b*)
             b) The reason (v. 3*c*)
    B. The Lord Sustains All Believers (v. 4)
        1. The position of believers (v. 4*a*)
        2. The power of God (v. 4*b*)
            a) John 10:28-29
            b) Romans 8:35-39
            c) John 6:37
            d) Jude 24-25
            e) 1 Peter 1:5-6

Introduction

The Lord is concerned about how Christians treat one another. In Matthew 18:6 Jesus tells His disciples, "Whosoever shall offend one of these little ones who believe in me, it were better for him that a millstone were hanged about his neck, and that he were drowned in the depth of the sea." Jesus was not talking about infants but about believers. He likens believers to little children. From verse 6 we learn that how we treat one another as Christians is a serious matter. In verse 7 Jesus says, "Woe unto the world because of offenses!" We expect the unregenerate world to offend believers, but we don't expect believers to do that. Then in verses 8-9 the Lord uses two familiar proverbial statements of His day to emphasize the point: "If thy hand or thy foot offend thee, cut it off. . . . If thine eye offend thee, pluck it out."

If you're led into sin by your hand or your foot, you'd be better off without them. The Lord's point is that sin must be dealt with drastically. We must be careful not to offend another believer. If we find we are doing that, we must take drastic measures to stop. In verse 10 Jesus wraps up the thought by saying, "Take heed that ye despise not one of these little ones; for I say unto you that in heaven their angels do always behold the face of my Father, who is in heaven." You don't want to be at odds with the holy angels and God the Father! In those verses our Lord established an important truth: we must take great care not to offend or look down on other believers.

Review

Paul picks up the same theme in Romans 14. His great concern is that believers learn how to get along. We are all aware that sin causes a rift in the fellowship of the church. But another area that creates conflict is the struggle of strong and weak believers over preferential issues. A great diversity of people is brought together in the church. There exists the potential for clash when preferences for external forms of worship or life-styles differ. Paul focuses on two sets of believers in his discussion: the weak and the strong. Disharmony results when the strong despise the weak for being small-minded and the weak condemn the strong for abusing their liberty.

To help us understand how strong and weak believers are to get along, Paul makes four points in Romans 14:1–15:13. The first point is the matter of receiving one another with understanding.

I. THE RECEPTION (v. 1; see pp. 15-25)

"Him that is weak in the faith receive ye, but not to doubtful disputations."

Paul told the strong to embrace the unemancipated into their fellowship instead of passing judgment on them. Then he told them why.

II. THE REASONS (vv. 2-12)

A. The Lord Receives All Believers (vv. 2-3)

1. Paul's generic description (v. 2)

   "One believeth that he may eat all things: another, who is weak, eateth herbs."

   One who is strong in the faith believes he can eat all things. He doesn't have any dietary constraints—he's not bound by the Mosaic dietary laws. However, there are others, who, being weak, eat only vegetables.

   a) Of the strong

   The strong Christian believes he can eat everything. But is he right? Can he eat everything?

   (1) 1 Timothy 4:4-5—"Every creature of God is good, and nothing is to be refused, if it is received with thanksgiving; for it is sanctified by the word of God and prayer." Paul made that statement in response to those who forbade others from eating certain foods.

   (2) Acts 10:15—After the Lord declared all animals clean, He told Peter, "What God hath cleansed, that call not thou common."

   The strong believer is right—you can eat anything, at least anything that is not injurious to your body. There are no dietary restrictions. We are not under the ceremonial laws of Moses. Every so often I hear some churches say believers shouldn't eat anything that was considered unclean in the Old Covenant. But that's not true. There are no such restraints in the New Covenant.

Paul in verse 2 may have been referring to strong Jewish believers, who were not burdened by eating pork or having their food cooked a certain way. He may also have been referring to strong Gentile believers who understood that food offered to idols was not important because an idol is nothing.

b) Of the weak

(1) Abstinence from vegetables

According to Paul's analysis in verse 2, the weak believer ate only vegetables. Based on history, we know that neither Jews or Gentiles had significant restrictions on eating vegetables. However, we do know vegetables were offered to idols as well as meat. The best interpretation is that Paul had in mind a particular Jewish group that was fearful of eating either meat offered to idols or meat that was unclean by their standards. So they opted for vegetables as the easiest way to avoid any problems. Some segments of the Essenes, the Jewish monastic sect that wrote the Dead Sea Scrolls, appear to have been vegetarian.

(2) Abstinence from drink

In Romans 14:17 Paul addresses food and drink. Apparently some also abstained from drink. This was probably not a Jewish issue because the wine the Jews drank was diluted with water. Paul may have been referring to a Gentile Christian with a Bacchanalian past, having once participated in worship of false gods in a drunken stupor. Also, some of the Essenes practiced total abstinence.

Paul wasn't trying to identify every person or group; he was merely pointing out that for whatever reason, some believers were preoccupied with what they ate while others weren't. His description in verse 2 is generic— some are free to enjoy their liberty, whereas others remain bound by the past and cannot.

2. Paul's specific injunction (v. 3)

   a) The restriction (v. 3a-b)

      (1) For the strong (v. 3a)

      "Let not him that eateth despise him that eateth not."

      The Greek word translated "despise" means "to treat someone as nothing" or "to look at someone with disdain or contempt." The strong believer should not look with contempt on one who doesn't fully understand his freedom in Christ. Sad to say, the church is full of liberated brethren who want to condemn those who are more confined in their thinking. I see that tendency in the church, and I sense that tendency in myself. When we come across believers who want to subject us to a list of unnecessary rules, we're tempted to view them with contempt.

      (2) For the weak (v. 3b)

      "Let not him who eateth not [the weak believer] judge [Gk., *krinō*, "condemn"] him that eateth."

      Weak believers have a tendency to condemn the strong because they don't understand their freedom in Christ. Some are afraid to venture outside the bounds of legalism because they believe they will lose control. I faced that kind of environment in college. The administrators were under the assumption that if they allowed the students any freedom, they'd go off the deep end. They wanted to keep everyone safe. When they did see someone who lived out his liberty in Christ and wasn't confined by the rules, they assumed there was sin in his life. They were abiding by the external and artificial standards they saw as indicators of true spirituality.

      Within the church of Jesus Christ are those who do not understand their freedom in Christ and condemn those who do. Those who understand their freedom tend to despise those who don't. The unity of the church was a vital issue to Paul. He said, "Ye may with one mind and one mouth glorify God" (Rom. 15:6).

b) The reason (v. 3*c*)

"God hath received him."

Who are we not to receive whom God has received? Although the word *him* in verse 3 is nearer to the phrase that discusses the weak's condemnation of the strong, we don't need to limit it to that. Neither are we to condemn or despise the other.

If you understand your liberty in Christ yet have a tendency to condemn a fellow believer for being legalistic, remember that God has received him through his faith in Christ. If you tend toward legalism and see a fellow believer who doesn't adhere to the rules that you do, don't condemn him, because God has received him, too. Since the Lord receives the weak, we ought to receive the weak. Since the Lord receives the strong, we ought to receive the strong. We have to learn to work together.

B. The Lord Sustains All Believers (v. 4)

The strong tend to despise the weak, and the weak tend to condemn the strong. To justify our concern—whichever it might be—we believe the other believer is in danger of falling away from the faith. The strong fear the weak will eventually despair of the Christian life with all the rigidity they impose on it. However, the weak fear the strong are going too far away from what God desires. Both groups fear spiritual disaster.

1. The position of believers (v. 4*a*)

"Who art thou that judgeth another man's servant [Gk., *oiketēs*, "a household slave"]? To his own master he standeth or falleth."

Paul questioned any believer's right to evaluate someone else's servant. Another's opinion doesn't improve or impair that servant's position before his own master. Judgment by an outsider is irrelevant. That's why Paul said, "Let a man so account of us, as of the ministers of Christ, and stewards of the mysteries of God. . . . But with me it is a very small thing that I should be judged of you, or of man's judgment; yea, I judge not my own self. For I know nothing against myself, yet am I not hereby justified; but he that judgeth me is the Lord" (1 Cor. 4:1, 3-4).

Paul uses the phrase "his own" (Gk., *idios*) for emphasis. Before his own master a servant stands or falls. Who is the master of the weak? The Lord. Who is the master of the strong? The Lord. Christ's own evaluation of a believer is what matters. He will decide whether a believer is doing right or wrong.

2. The power of God (v. 4*b*)

"Yea, he shall be held up; for God is able to make him stand."

If a person truly belongs to the Lord, you don't need to worry about him. Even believers who are bound by many constraints are useful to God. They may not enjoy the fullness of their liberty, but the Lord is able to make them stand. Why? Because whomever He justifies—whether strong or weak—He eventually glorifies (Rom. 8:30). According to the textual variants, the best rendering of verse 4 is, "He shall be held up for the Lord is able to make him stand." You don't need to worry about a believer's collapsing, because God will make him stand.

The Greek word translated "is able" is a form of *dunamis,* the source of the English word *dynamite.* God is powerful!

a) John 10:28-29—Jesus said, "Neither shall any man pluck them out of my hand. My Father, who gave them to me, is greater than all, and no man is able to pluck them out of my Father's hand."

b) Romans 8:35-39—Nothing can separate us from the love of Christ, because those whom He predestined He will bring to glory (vv. 29-31).

c) John 6:37—Jesus said, "All that the Father giveth me shall come to me, and him that cometh to me I will in no wise cast out."

d) Jude 24-25—Jude said, "Now unto him that is able to keep you from falling . . . to the only wise God, our Savior."

e) 1 Peter 1:5-6—Peter said that we "are kept by the power of God through faith unto salvation ready to be revealed in the last time. In this ye greatly rejoice."

We don't need to fear that legalistic believers or liberated believers will fall away.

Subtle Evidence

In Romans 14:3 Paul says that God has received both the weak and strong. In verse 4 he says that God is able to make them stand. In verse 6 he says, "He that regardeth the day, regardeth it unto the Lord. . . . He that eateth, eateth to the Lord; for he giveth God thanks; and he that eateth not, to the Lord he eateth not, and giveth God thanks." In verse 8 Paul uses the word *Lord* three times. And in verse 9 he identifies Christ as the Lord. That interchange of Lord, Christ, and God is great subtle proof of the deity of Jesus Christ.

C. The Lord Is Sovereign over All Believers (vv. 5-9)

The Motives of the Strong and Weak

Paul's point in verses 5-9 is that even though the practices of the strong and weak vary, their motives are the same. Why does a weak believer keep the law and tradition? Because he believes in his heart that he is pleasing the Lord. Why does a strong believer

35

enjoy the freedoms he's been given in Christ? Because he believes in his heart that he is pleasing the Lord.

Being weak in the faith is not synonymous with being disobedient or sinful. A weak believer can be spiritual. Spirituality is an absolute. At any moment you can be either spiritual or fleshy. You walk either by the Spirit or your flesh. Maturity is the end product of spirituality.

There are weak Christians coming out of a religious tradition who are spiritually minded. They want to serve God with all their heart and soul, but they don't understand their freedoms in Christ. And some of those who do understand can be fleshy. Therefore we can't assume those who are weak in the faith do not desire to please the Lord.

1. The manifestation of a good conscience (v. 5a)

"One man esteemeth one day above another; another esteemeth every day alike."

If a believer came out of Judaism, he would probably consider some days more important than others, such as the Sabbath, feast days, and holy days. A similar veneration of days was part of paganism as well.

a) Elements of an old system

The veneration of days is a weakness. In Colossians 2:16 Paul says, "Let no man, therefore, judge you . . . in respect of a feast day, or of the new moon, or of a sabbath day." In Galatians 4:9 he refers to such things as "beggarly elements." They are part of an old system. The New Covenant frees us from having to observe special days.

b) Examples of a cultural system

When I was a boy, my family would come home from church, eat a big dinner, and then sit around. We could not play catch, read the paper or a magazine, watch television, or listen to the radio. Some people view

Sunday in that manner. Some people regard the day; some people don't. It was so then; it is so today.

2. The maintenance of a good conscience (v. 5*b*)

"Let every man be fully persuaded in his own mind."

a) Deferring to one's own conscience

Paul said to do whatever you think you ought to do. Why? Because the veneration of days is not a moral issue. The Sabbath has been set aside. Paul is not concerned with Sabbaths and feast days, but he is concerned that people not train themselves to violate their consciences. If your conscience tells you to keep a certain day, then keep it. If you train yourself to ignore your conscience, you will have problems. The Spirit of God leads subjectively through a person's conscience. Paul does not want anyone to have a conscience seared with a hot iron (1 Tim. 4:2)—a scarred conscience insensitive to truth and the prodding of God's Spirit.

Don't train your conscience to do wrong. If your conscience tells you to abide by certain preferential traditions and taboos, then do so if you believe it pleases the Lord. Don't let anyone tell you not to. Some people believe that everything God wants you to know about His will is in the Bible. I believe that belief ignores some things that Scripture teaches about keeping a pure conscience so that God's Spirit can subjectively lead you.

b) Deferring to another's conscience

First Corinthians 8:7 says, "There is not in every man that knowledge; for some with conscience of the idol unto this hour eat it as a thing offered unto an idol, and their conscience, being weak, is defiled." In verse 8 Paul says that if a believer is bothered by eating food offered to an idol, then don't make him eat it. In verse 9 he says, "Take heed lest by any means this liberty of yours become a stumbling block to them that are weak."

I often hear liberated believers criticizing the weak for their attachment to something they need no longer hold to. But by criticizing the weak, the strong are pressuring them into doing something that will defile their conscience. That will make the weak feel guilty and drive them deeper into legalism. We must be patient for the Spirit of God, the Word of God, and the community of believers to bring the weak to maturity. Paul continues in 1 Corinthians 8:11, "Through thy knowledge shall the weak brother perish, for whom Christ died?" Do you want to destroy a weaker believer by forcing him to abuse his conscience? No. The conscience is an important tool in the hands of God. Acts 23:1 says that "Paul, earnestly beholding the council, said, Men and brethren, I have lived in all good conscience before God." Paul not only obeyed the Word but also did what he believed the Spirit of God prompted him to do in his conscience.

3. The motives of a good conscience (vv. 6-7)

   a) Giving thanks to God (v. 6)

      "He that regardeth the day, regardeth it unto the Lord. . . . He that eateth, eateth to the Lord; for he giveth God thanks; and he that eateth not, to the Lord he eateth not, and giveth God thanks."

      The strong brother eats everything in sight and thanks the Lord for his freedom. The weak brother eats according to his ceremonial diet and thanks the Lord that he makes a sacrifice on His behalf. In either case the believer thanks the Lord, so the motive is the same.

   b) Doing what pleases God (v. 7)

      "None of us liveth to himself, and no man dieth to himself."

      Paul is saying that whether weak or strong, we do what we do for the Lord, not for ourselves. That's the way it should be with Christians. We submitted to His lordship when we became Christians—we left our self-centered life behind. Now our most basic desire is to serve Him.

4. The manager of a good conscience (vv. 8-9)

   a) The affirmation of Christ's lordship (v. 8)

   "Whether we live, we live unto the Lord; and whether we die, we die unto the Lord; whether we live, therefore, or die, we are the Lord's."

   The Greek text literally says, "To the Lord we live; to the Lord we die." We live for Him; someday we'll die for Him—whether weak or strong, newborn Christian infants or mature believers.

   The last phrase of verse 9—"we are the Lord's"—is one of the greatest injunctions to holy living in the Bible. Every Christian is subject to the unconditional sovereignty of God. We are the Lord's; we are His possession. First Corinthians 6:19-20 says, "Know ye not that . . . ye are not your own? For ye are bought with a price." I'm not my own, so I don't live to myself, and I don't die to myself. I am His, so I live to Him, and I'll die to Him. All believers have the same relationship to the Lord; we all serve the sovereign Lord we have embraced as our Redeemer. If we're weak and we limit ourselves to living a certain way, we do so because we believe we are pleasing Him. If we enjoy our freedom in Christ, we do so because we believe we are pleasing Him. Since those are matters of preference and not sin, let's not cause a rift in the church over them.

   Romans 14:8 brings much to bear on the issue of the lordship of Christ. A true Christian longs to submit to Christ's lordship. First Corinthians 15:23 includes the short phrase "they that are Christ's." The greatest injunction to holy living is that we are the Lord's. We belong to Him, whether weak or strong. Some would have us believe that weak believers accept Jesus as their Savior but not as their Lord. Although a weak believer may not understand all that his new life in Christ means, he understands the basics of the Chris-

39

tian life—and nothing is more basic than the lordship of Christ in the believer's life. In all the years I've known Christ, there has never been a time when I didn't sense a tremendous weight of responsibility to obey Him.

b) The accomplishment of Christ's death (v. 9)

"To this end Christ both died, and rose, and revived, that he might be Lord both of the dead and living."

Scripture specifically states that Jesus died to be Lord (as opposed to Savior). It is hard for me to conceive how people can believe that one can have Jesus as Savior yet not have any sense of submission to His lordship. Jesus died and rose that He might be lord. The Greek verb *kurieuō* is translated "might be Lord." The noun form is *kurios*, the common word for "Lord." Jesus died and rose to be lord of both the living and the dead. The dead refers to saints already in glory. Christ died to reign over the saints in His presence and the saints still on earth. He has dominion over all creation and a special mediatorial function on behalf of His own people (Heb. 2:17; 7:25). It is impossible to deny the lordship of Jesus Christ without denying His work on the cross.

D. The Lord Alone Will Judge All Believers (vv. 10-12)

1. The imperative questions (v. 10*a-b*)

a) Why do the weak judge the strong? (v. 10*a*)

"Why dost thou judge thy brother?"

b) Why do the strong despise the weak? (v. 10*b*)

"Or why dost thou set at nought thy brother?"

2. The inevitable judgment (vv. 10c-12)

   a) All will stand in judgment (v. 10c)

   "We shall all stand before the judgment seat of Christ [God]."

   The Greek text says "God" [*theou*] not "Christ." It is in 2 Corinthians 5:10 where it is called the judgment seat of Christ. Those two verses are more evidence of the deity of Christ because He is spoken of interchangeably with God. First Corinthians 3:12-13 says that when we stand before the judgment seat our works will be put on display, whether gold, silver, precious stones, wood, hay, or stubble. First Corinthians 4:5 says the Lord "will bring to light the hidden things of darkness, and will make manifest the counsels of the hearts; and then shall every man have praise of God."

   b) All will bow in judgment (v. 11)

   "It is written, As I live, saith the Lord, every knee shall bow to me, and every tongue shall confess to God."

   That is a quote from Isaiah 45:23. Paul used a portion of that same verse in Philippians 2:10-11. Every one of us at one point in the future will bow before the judgment seat of God. When we judge others, we are playing God—and that's a blasphemous thing to do.

   c) All will give account in judgment (v. 12)

   "So, then, every one of us shall give account of himself to God."

   There will be a time for an accounting. We will all stand before God and have our works examined. Then we'll receive the praise and the reward God has planned to give us.

41

Conclusion

Why should we open our arms and receive each other? Because God receives us. He holds us up. He is sovereign, and ultimately He alone has the right to judge us. Many conflicts in the church arise over non-essentials, but they can be stopped if we'll receive one another. Drop unnecessary criticism. Let the Lord be the judge. It's better that we should love one another.

Focusing on the Facts

1. What important truth does Jesus establish in Matthew 18:6-10 (see pp. 28-29)?
2. Is it right for the strong believer to eat anything he wants? Why or why not (see p. 30)?
3. What group of people does Paul probably have in mind in Romans 14:2 when he says that they eat only vegetables (see p. 31)?
4. What is Paul's specific injunction for the strong in Romans 14:3? What was his specific injunction for the weak (see p. 32)?
5. What was Paul's reason for giving those injunctions (see p. 33)?
6. Explain how the weak and the strong believe each other will fall away (see p. 33).
7. Who is master of both the strong and weak believer? Why is that important (see p. 34)?
8. Why shouldn't we worry about a believer's collapsing (Rom. 14:4; see p. 34)?
9. How secure is the believer in Christ? Cite some verses to support your answer (see pp. 34-35).
10. What motivates both the weak and strong believer to act the way they do (see pp. 35-36)?
11. Why did Paul say that a person ought to regard certain days if that's what his conscience leads him to do (see p. 37)?
12. What might strong Christians pressure their weaker brothers into doing by criticizing them for their beliefs (see p. 38)?
13. What should be the motive of every believer (Rom. 14:7; see pp. 38-39)?
14. Why shouldn't believers live for themselves (see pp. 39-40)?
15. According to Romans 14:9, why did Christ die and rise from the dead (see p. 40)?

16. What do people effectively deny when they deny the lordship of Christ (see p. 40)?
17. What will happen to all believers when they are brought before the judgment seat of God (see p. 41)?

Pondering the Principles

1. Look up the following verses: Psalm 37:17, 24, 28; John 10:28-30; Romans 8:31-39; Hebrews 7:25; and Jude 24. In your own words, record what those verses tell you about your eternal security. How does that help you to view the security of other believers? The next time you are tempted to judge the ultimate outcome of a believer who holds to a different preference in some non-moral area, what will you do?

2. Read Romans 14:8-9, and review the section on the manager of a good conscience (see pp. 39-40). Do you treat Christ as lord of your life, or do you thank Him for your salvation and do what you want? In light of Paul's teaching, how do you need to change your perception of your relationship to Christ? What do you need to change in terms of your obedience to Christ? Make the commitment this week to focus your time and energy on those activities that will be pleasing to Him.

3
Building Up One Another Without Offending—Part 1

Outline

Introduction
A. Abstaining from Our Liberty in Christ
    1. Developing conformity
    2. Displaying love
B. Abusing Our Liberty in Christ
    1. Self-deception
       a) An addiction to alcohol
       b) An addiction to television
       c) An addiction to golf
    2. Self-destruction
       a) 1 Corinthians 6:12
       b) 1 Corinthians 10:23
    3. Self-bondage
    4. Self-retardation

Lesson
  I. Don't Cause Your Brother to Stumble (v. 13)
    A. Reaffirming God's Sovereignty
    B. Removing Stumbling Blocks
      1. Scriptural instruction
      2. Contemporary illustrations
        a) Drinking
        b) Dancing
 II. Don't Grieve Your Brother (vv. 14-15*a*)
    A. The Absence of Sin (v. 14*a*)
      1. 1 Timothy 4:3-4
      2. Titus 1:15
      3. Mark 7:15
      4. Acts 10:13-15

Introduction

Jesus Christ granted us great liberty in the New Covenant. We are not encumbered by the Old Testament ceremonial law. We are free to enjoy all the good gifts God has created for us, but we are not free to sin. As recipients of the blessings of the New Covenant, we are free to enjoy all that God has provided without any restrictions in terms of non-moral issues. But certain believers attempt to convince us that we're not free to eat or drink certain things. Others tell us our recreation is limited. Some tell us we cannot watch television or movies. Others tell us that playing cards are evil. Some tell us that a man should not let his hair grow over his ears or wear a beard. All those things have nothing to do with what Scripture clearly delineates as sin. They are neutral—neither right or wrong according to Scripture—and are the elements of Christian liberty.

To understand how we should react to neutral things, we need instruction from the Word of God. In the church of Jesus Christ are strong believers who understand their freedom and can enjoy the good gifts God has given them. However, they need to be careful not to abuse that freedom in a sinful way. There are also weak believers, who bring into their Christian lives taboos and scruples from their previous backgrounds. They believe some neutral things are not permissible. Therefore, the potential for conflict exists in the church between those who want to exercise their freedom and those who want to limit their freedom.

Paul's concern is that this conflict will disrupt the unity of the church, so he addresses the issue of personal preferences in Romans 14:1–15:13. Paul divides his discussion into four categories. We have already looked at the first one (see pp. 15-42). The second one we will examine is building up one another without offending.

A. Abstaining from Our Liberty in Christ

Is it necessary to eat or drink or do whatever your liberty allows to prove you are strong? No. In fact, you will demonstrate greater spiritual strength when you don't exercise your liberty for the sake of weaker believers. Just because you possess liberty doesn't mean you have to exercise it. When a weak believer abstains from his liberty, it reflects his lack of understanding. When a strong believer abstains from his liberty, it reflects his love for a weaker brother. No believer should flaunt his freedom to prove he is strong, and no believer should be pressed into exercising freedom to prove he is strong when he is not. The weaker believer should abstain out of his unbelief, and the stronger believer should abstain out of love.

1. Developing conformity

Conformity develops in a church when two things happen: the weaker believers set limitations on their liberties because their consciences don't allow them to exercise them, and the stronger believers set up the same limitations out of love for the weaker believers. Conformity develops as the strong confine themselves to what will be tolerated by the weak. They will build relationships with the weak that eventually will strengthen them and widen their scope of liberty.

2. Displaying love

Our freedom has been given to us by God. Whether we exercise it is another matter. I'm free to do things I never do because I want to demonstrate my love for the weak. My liberty is vertical. I enjoy my liberty before the Lord. But the exercise of my liberty is horizontal—between myself and another person—and that is limited by my love. Paul's concern is to teach the strong to restrain their liberty for love's sake, making sure they don't flaunt it before others.

A commentator has said that there is a great difference between Christian liberty and the use of Christian liberty. Christian liberty is an internal thing—it belongs to the mind and the conscience and has a direct reference to God. The issue of Christian liberty is an external thing—it belongs to conduct and has reference to man. We should not give up our liberty since our liberty grows out of the teaching of the Word of God and our consciences, which are governed by the Lord. We should be willing to die for the maintenance of our liberty. But we should forgo the display of our liberty if it will cause the weak to stumble.

We have liberty in Christ, but we prove our strength not by flaunting our liberty but by controlling it. We need to discern those believers who are weak and restrain our liberty to bring it in line with their weaknesses. In gaining their love we are able to move them toward a greater understanding of liberty.

B. Abusing Our Liberty in Christ

The Bible places restraints on our liberty. Paul deals with some of them in Romans 14:13-23, but there are others elsewhere in the Bible.

1. Self-deception

The exercise of our liberty is certainly not for the purpose of self-deception. In 1 Peter 2:16 Peter tells believers not to use their liberty as a cloak for their wickedness.

a) An addiction to alcohol

Suppose you are addicted to alcohol. That is sin, according to the Word of God. But to cloak your problem, you flaunt the fact that you are free in Christ to drink, because drinking alcohol is not inherently wicked in and of itself. You are not to do that.

b) An addiction to television

Suppose you watch television all the time, allowing whatever garbage that parades across the screen to parade through your mind. If anyone calls it to your attention, don't say, "But I'm free in Christ! Besides, TV is just mere electrical impulses." Don't use your liberty in Christ to cloak what is basically a sinful preoccupation—something that is sucking the life out of your spiritual development.

c) An addiction to golf

Suppose you like to play golf on Sunday mornings. You might say, "I'm free; I'm worshiping God in creation instead of in church." There's nothing inherently evil about golf. But claiming your freedom in that area is nothing but a cloak to cover the wickedness of a heart that is not interested in worshiping God.

2. Self-destruction

Self-destruction goes against the intentions of our liberty in Christ. There's nothing inherently evil in a tobacco plant, but when you allow cigarettes to destroy your health and dominate your life, you allow a nonmoral thing to become the source of your self-destruction. I know a man who loved drinking beer so much that he left the church rather than set aside his liberty in Christ. He claimed it was his freedom to drink; the truth is that it was self-destructive.

a) 1 Corinthians 6:12—Paul says, "All things are lawful unto me." He doesn't mean unlawful things are lawful; he means all things that aren't unlawful are lawful. He continues, "But all things are not expedient." Paul is saying that even though all things are lawful, they aren't all beneficial. If you smoke cigarettes they will hurt you. Smoking isn't immoral, but it isn't smart. You could say the same thing about movies or

49

television. When they become something that destroys a person, they are unlawful.

About twenty years ago a well-known evangelist decided to play golf often. Eventually he was playing golf for $4,000 a game. It destroyed him. He lost everything, including his ministry. There's nothing inherently evil in playing golf, but when it results in self-destruction it is an abuse of freedom.

b) 1 Corinthians 10:23—Paul repeats the same idea in this verse: "All things are lawful for me, but all things are not expedient." It doesn't make sense to engage in something I cannot control.

3. Self-bondage

The purpose of Christian liberty is not to bring you under the control of something so that you become its slave, yet that can happen. Some people are controlled by chocolate. Some people are controlled by soap operas—if they can't get home to see the next serial, they're miserable. Those people are slaves; they've been brought into bondage. First Corinthians 6:12 says, "All things are lawful for me, but I will not be brought under the power of [lit., "be entangled by"] any."

Man was created to be the king of the earth. He was created and then given dominion. But because of man's fall, things now hold dominion over him. People can be controlled by cigarettes or food. Some people literally live to eat. In a fallen world, God's good gifts to us can become our master.

4. Self-retardation

In 1 Corinthians 10:23 Paul says, "All things are lawful for me, but all things edify not." Our freedom is not for the purpose of doing things that tear us down. Since I value my relationship to the Lord, I want to avoid anything that tears me down. There may be things in your life that tear you down spiritually because they keep you away from the people of God. Television or movies may keep you away from studying God's Word. We do

50

not have freedom to engage in an activity that tears us down.

I have liberty in Christ. But my liberty is not for the sake of self-deception—not to cloak my vice. It is not for self-destruction—not to get me into habits that ultimately destroy my effectiveness for God. It is not for self-bondage—not so I can be controlled by something. And it is not for self-retardation—not so that whatever I engage in pulls me down spiritually.

Those are all personal restraints, but in Romans 14:13-23 Paul talks about how the abuse of Christian liberty affects my brothers and sisters in Christ. That ultimately affects the church. Paul's concern is how Christians are to build up other Christians without offending. That calls for limiting our exercise of liberty. Don't let anyone threaten your liberty by binding your conscience to things that are not in themselves evil. But at the same time, don't flaunt your liberty to prove you're strong. That may result in your own bondage or in division among the fellowship of believers.

How do we avoid offending each other? The key is in Romans 14:15: "Walkest thou not in love?" You need to be sure that the exercise of your liberty is not unloving and insensitive to other believers. The objective of a strong believer in the church of Christ is to conduct himself in love toward a weaker brother.

Lesson

I. DON'T CAUSE YOUR BROTHER TO STUMBLE (v. 13)

"Let us not, therefore, judge one another any more; but judge this, rather: that no man put a stumbling block or an occasion to fall in his brother's way."

A. Reaffirming God's Sovereignty

The word *therefore* takes us back to the first twelve verses of Romans 14. Since the Lord receives every Christian—whether weak or strong—since He is able to hold up both strong and weak, since He is sovereign over each, and since the Lord is the final judge, we are not to judge one another. The weak are not to judge the strong because they think they are abusing their freedom, nor are the strong to condemn the weak for their lack of faith and small-mindedness.

B. Removing Stumbling Blocks

Paul tells us we do have a decision to make. And he puts it in the form of an aorist imperative, which calls for action. Our decision should be not only to stop judging one another but also to stop putting stumbling blocks in the way of others. That has to be the preoccupation of our lives. Picture a brother and sister walking along the path of the Christian life; then someone puts something in their path to cause them to fall. We don't want to stop a fellow believer in his spiritual progress by causing him to fall into sin.

1. Scriptural instruction

In 1 Corinthians 8 Paul deals with some of the Gentiles in Corinth who had trouble eating or drinking what had been offered to idols. Some of the more liberated brethren were not concerned about that because they knew an idol was nothing; therefore anything offered to nothing is nothing. So there was potential for conflict in the church. In verse 9 Paul says, "Take heed lest by any means this liberty of yours become a stumbling block to them that are weak." How does that happen? Paul continues, "For if any man see thee, who hast knowledge, sitting at the table in the idol's temple, shall not the conscience of him who is weak be emboldened to eat those things which are offered to idols, and through thy knowledge shall the weak brother perish, for whom Christ died?" (vv. 10-11).

When you exercise your freedom, and your brother sees that you are free to do what he thinks is wrong, he might be tempted to follow your example. But when he does, his conscience is guilty because he truly believes it is wrong. So the strong believer has inadvertently created a guilty conscience in the weak brother, causing him to stumble. It is possible the weaker brother might return into an old pattern of sin. He might go back to an idol feast and get caught up in the orgy and debauchery of it, with disastrous results.

2. Contemporary illustrations

   a) Drinking

   People often ask me if I drink alcoholic beverages. I don't for many reasons. One reason is that the last thing I want to do is give someone the idea that ministers and other servants of God are free to drink alcohol. When someone who was an alcoholic before he came to Christ thinks he is free to drink because he has been emboldened by what he has seen someone else do, he could return to the pit of his drunkenness. We must not cause someone else to stumble.

   b) Dancing

   People also ask me if I dance. Because I want to be a good example, I choose to set aside certain things, like dancing, that some believers might object to.

   My parents reared me not to dance. In fact, few Christians used to dance. This saying was popular in Christian circles: "You don't want to dance because people who go to dances later go out and neck."

   When I was in the ninth grade we had a class dance. A girl came up to me and said, "I want you to dance with me." I said, "No. You don't want me to dance with you. I don't dance—I don't even know how to dance." She became upset. She told one of the teachers, who happened to be my algebra teacher. The teacher told me that if I wasn't on that dance floor in five minutes I would flunk algebra. If you could see my ninth-grade transcript from North Downey Junior High, you would see I received an "F" for algebra. I didn't dance. (I believe I only had a "D" at the time, anyway!)

   I believe the limitations most Christians impose on dancing are based on the things associated with its environment. With the exception of folk dances, which possess inherent beauty and dignity, most dancing environments are not the kind that stimulate a weak believer to godliness. As a strong Christian, you might be able to go dancing with your wife, but many believers wouldn't be able to. To them it would be a tremendous stumbling block.

When you trip up a believer and cause him to fall, you have acted in less than a loving manner. To build up a believer without offending him you must be sure not to do anything that might tempt him to do something that could cause him to fall.

II. DON'T GRIEVE YOUR BROTHER (vv. 14-15a)

A. The Absence of Sin (v. 14a)

"I know, and am persuaded by the Lord Jesus, that there is nothing unclean of itself."

Paul states emphatically that he didn't receive his teaching by hearsay; he received it directly from his personal, intimate communion with the Lord Jesus Christ. That was the unique privilege of writers of Scripture.

Paul is telling believers not to go to the other extreme and give up their liberty entirely. He wants them to understand and enjoy their liberty. After all, the strong are correct: sin does not reside in food, drink, film, electronics, games, or recreation.

1. 1 Timothy 4:3-4—Paul said that all things, including food, are to be received with thanksgiving. Don't allow anyone tell you to abstain from certain foods.

2. Titus 1:15—Paul said, "Unto the pure all things are pure, but unto them that are defiled and unbelieving is nothing pure; but even their mind and conscience is defiled."

3. Mark 7:15—Jesus said, "There is nothing from outside of a man that, entering into him, can defile him; but the things which come out of him, those are they that defile the man."

4. Acts 10:13-15—After Peter saw a sheet containing unclean animals descend from heaven, the Lord said, "Rise, Peter; kill, and eat [God was setting aside the Old Covenant dietary laws]. But Peter said, Not so, Lord; for I have never eaten anything that is common or unclean. And the voice spoke unto him again the second time, What God hath cleansed, that call not thou common." The Greek word translated "unclean" means "common," but it came to mean "impure" or "evil."

B. The Attitude of Believers (vv. 14b-15a)

1. The rejection by the weak (v. 14b)

"But to him that esteemeth anything to be unclean, to him it is unclean."

Not everyone can handle everything that is acceptable. In 1 Corinthians 8:7 Paul says, "There is not in every man that knowledge [that an idol is nothing]; for some with conscience of the idol unto this hour eat it as a thing offered unto an idol, and their conscience being weak, is defiled." A godly person who understands his liberty in Christ should not be dissuaded from exercising it, but those who are ignorant of their liberties shouldn't be shown a pattern of behavior that will cause them to stumble. They shouldn't be encouraged to violate their consciences; they need an example of love that meets them on their own ground.

a) Developing a guilty conscience

I don't believe Paul is teaching that sin is subjective—that it is only what you believe it is. Sin is explicitly defined in Scripture. But Paul is not talking about those things that are inherently sinful. If a person believes it is a sin to do something that isn't inherently sinful, yet does it, he will have a guilty conscience.

One weakness I have is how I spend my time. It's hard for me to relax. There are some days when I decide to do nothing for a couple of hours, but I can hardly get through those hours because I have a guilty conscience. People say, "Why do you feel guilty?

Everyone is entitled to a few hours without being encumbered with some task." But that weakness in me helps me understand what the weaker believer's conscience is like.

I overheard someone say, "I never miss a morning without having my personal devotions." Another individual replied, "You need to stop doing that so you can prove you're not a legalist. Skip a few days." The person took that advice and suffered tremendously from a guilty conscience. Is it a sin not to have your morning devotions? It isn't addressed as such in the Bible. But if your conscience tells you it is wrong to skip devotions, and you do, then you will suffer with a guilty conscience.

b) Desiring a clean conscience

Jamieson, Fausset, and Brown's commentary remarks, "Whatever tends to make anyone violate his conscience tends to the destruction of his soul; and he who helps, whether wittingly or no, to bring about the one is guilty of aiding to accomplish the other" (*Commentary Practical and Explanatory on the Whole Bible* [Grand Rapids, Mich.: Zondervan, n.d.], p. 1178). The Lord wants you to have a clean conscience. You should never train yourself to violate or ignore your conscience. That would be training yourself to ignore the instrument through which the Spirit of God subjectively leads you. Desire to have a conscience void of offense toward God (Acts 24:16). When a stronger believer tempts a weaker believer to violate his conscience, the weaker believer will have painful, bitter sorrow in his heart. Instead of helping him grow in his spiritual life, the stronger believer has caused him to be even more afraid of his liberty.

2. The responsibility of the strong (v. 15*a*)

"But if thy brother be grieved with thy food, now walkest thou not in love."

How would a weak believer be grieved? Simply by seeing a strong Christian do what he believed was wrong.

If you are strongly convinced that something is wrong, and you see a strong believer do it, you will be grieved over his seeming abuse of liberty. But in the context of Romans 14, I believe Paul is saying that the weaker believer is grieved not just because of that but because he thinks he must follow suit. But by following the instruction or example of the strong believer, he does what he believes is wrong and has to live with the remorse and guilt of his conscience. He forfeits the peace and joy of his Christian walk.

You need to set your life on a path that will not grieve others—that will not make them follow you into something their consciences tell them not to. That means you have to get close enough to each other to know where you stand on those issues. You have to know the hearts of the people around you so you can be sure to have an unselfish love for them.

III. DON'T DEVASTATE YOUR BROTHER (v. 15b)

"Destroy not him with thy food, for whom Christ died."

A. The Concept of Destruction

The Greek word translated "destroy" is *apollumi*, which means "to ruin." It is a strong and serious word. It is translated frequently as "perish." It can have several meanings:

1. Damnation

John 3:16 says, "God so loved the world, that he gave his only begotten Son, that whosoever believeth in Him should not perish, but have everlasting life." Second Peter 3:9 says God is "not willing that any should perish." Other verses using *apollumi* are Matthew 10:28, Luke 13:3, Romans 2:12, 2 Corinthians 4:3, and 2 Thessalonians 2:10. The word can have the meaning of eternal destruction when referring to unbelievers.

2. Death

Apollumi can also be a general term for the death or elimination of something.

a) 1 Corinthians 1:19—"It is written, I will destroy the wisdom of the wise, and will bring to nothing the understanding of the prudent." God will wipe out the folly of those who suppose themselves to be wise in their worldly philosophies.

b) 1 Corinthians 10:9-10—Paul said that the people of Israel were "destroyed by serpents." Then he said, "Neither murmur ye, as some of them also murmured, and were destroyed by the destroyer."

The word is used in this general sense also in Hebrews 1:11, James 1:11, and 1 Peter 1:7.

3. Spiritual loss

Apollumi is also used in Scripture to speak of believers. When it is so used, it has some latitude.

a) Matthew 18:14—Matthew 18 is a familiar chapter on the childlikeness of the believer. Verse 14 says, "It is not the will of your Father, who is in heaven, that one of these little ones should perish." That verse is part of a passage about not offending Christians. It is a great parallel to Romans 14. Matthew 18:6 says that true believers are like little children. Verse 3 says, "Except ye be converted, and become as little children, ye shall not enter into the kingdom of heaven." In verse 6 Jesus says that anyone who offends a believer would be better off drowned.

In verse 10 Jesus says, "Take heed that ye despise not [Gk., *kataphroneō*, "look down on"] one of these little ones; for I say unto you that in heaven their angels do always behold the face of my Father, who is in heaven." In verses 12-13 Jesus shows how concerned the Father and the angels are over believers: "If a man have an hundred sheep, and one of them be gone astray, doth he not leave the ninety and nine, and goeth into the mountains, and seeketh that which is gone astray? And if so be that he find it, verily I say unto you, he rejoiceth more over that sheep than over the ninety and nine which went not astray." God is the shepherd, and the sheep are His own.

Verse 14 says, "It is not the will of your Father, who is in heaven, that one of these little ones should perish."

Can you offend a believer to the degree that he will perish forever in hell? No. But he will suffer spiritual loss or experience disaster in his life. He could leave the church. He could lose his joy. He could lose even his effectiveness in ministry.

b) 1 Corinthians 8:11—Paul, speaking to believers, said, "Through thy knowledge shall the weak brother perish, for whom Christ died?" In context *apollumi* cannot mean eternal destruction; it must refer to suffering loss.

c) 2 John 8—John, addressing believers, said, "Look to yourselves, that we lose not those things which we have wrought, but that we receive a full reward." The same word is used to mean the loss of reward.

Apollumi, when used in reference to believers, indicates the loss of spiritual blessing. When you cause your brother to stumble, to grieve, or to lose spiritual blessing, you have not acted lovingly.

B. The Cause of Destruction

Romans 14:15 says, "Destroy not him *with thy food*" (emphasis added). Food was emblematic of their liberty. Paul was talking to a liberated Jew who would flaunt a pork chop in the face of a newly converted Jew, or a liberated Gentile who would eat meat offered to idols in front of a newly converted pagan. Why let something as unimportant as food do something as awful as causing spiritual loss for a weaker believer?

C. The Contrast of Destruction

Paul concluded by telling the strong not to plunge the weak, "for whom Christ died," into spiritual devastation (v. 15). That's a virtual repetition of 1 Corinthians 8:11. How could a strong believer treat in a loveless way someone for whom Christ died in an act of supreme love? What a contrast! Since Christ, the perfect Son of God, loved that weaker brother enough to die for him, shouldn't the strong believer, who is to emulate Christ, love his brother enough not to devastate his spirituality by insisting on his own liberty regardless of the circumstances?

Paul calls us to build up one another by not causing each other to stumble, to grieve, or to suffer spiritual loss.

Focusing on the Facts

1. Is it necessary for the strong believer to do whatever his liberty allows to prove he is strong? Explain (see p. 47).
2. When will conformity in the church develop (see p. 47)?
3. Describe the difference between having Christian liberty and using it (see pp. 47-48).
4. What are four common personal abuses of liberty? Describe each (see pp. 48-50).
5. What is the key point in Romans 14:13-23? Explain (see p. 51).
6. In what sense are we not to judge other believers (see p. 51)?
7. What should be the preoccupation of strong believers (Rom. 14:13; see p. 52)?
8. According to 1 Corinthians 8:9-11, how does a strong believer create a guilty conscience in a weak believer (see p. 52)?
9. What is Paul communicating in Romans 14:14*a* (see p. 54)?
10. Why shouldn't weak believers be encouraged to exercise their liberty against their better judgment (see p. 55)?
11. Why shouldn't a believer train himself to violate his conscience (see p. 56)?
12. How is a weak believer grieved by a strong believer (Rom. 14:15*a*; see pp. 56-57)?
13. What are the various meanings of the Greek word *apollumi* in Scripture (see pp. 57-59)?
14. What striking passage makes a great parallel to Romans 14? Explain its significance (see p. 58).

Pondering the Principles

1. Are you in danger of abusing your liberty to the point of harming yourself? Review the section on abusing Christian liberty

(see pp. 48-51). Be honest in your evaluation as you answer the following questions: Are you using your freedom to cloak sin? Are you participating in any activity that is either potentially harmful to your health or to your ministry? Are you involved in anything to the point that you have become a slave to it? Are you doing anything that might result in your being torn down spiritually? If you answered yes to any of those questions, you are abusing your liberty in Christ. Stop your involvement in those things. Limit your liberty for your own sake.

2. Are there people in your fellowship you may have hurt by exercising some of your freedoms in Christ? Have you caused a brother to stumble, to grieve, or to suffer spiritual loss? If so, then you need to show him your love by limiting your liberty. What kinds of things can you do to reach down to him at his level of maturity? Only when you see things from his level can you begin to encourage him through Scripture to release some of his inhibitions in exercising his freedoms in Christ. But be cautious. Don't encourage him beyond what he is able to handle. Better that you should love him where he is than force him beyond his secure position.

4
Building Up One Another Without Offending—Part 2

Outline

Review
I. Don't Cause Your Brother to Stumble (v. 13)
II. Don't Grieve Your Brother (vv. 14-15a)
III. Don't Devastate Your Brother (v. 15b)
    A. The Concept of Destruction
    B. The Cause of Destruction
    C. The Contrast of Destruction

Lesson
IV. Don't Forfeit Your Witness (vv. 16-19)
    A. The Christian Purpose (vv. 16-18)
        1. An authentic love (v. 16)
            a) A blasphemous problem
            b) A scriptural principle
        2. An appealing kingdom (v. 17)
            a) The non-essentials (v. 17a)
            b) The necessary elements (v. 17b)
                (1) Righteousness
                (2) Peace
                (3) Joy
        3. An acceptable servant (v. 18)
            a) To God
            b) To men
    B. The Christian Pursuit (v. 19)
        1. The things that make for peace
            a) 2 Corinthians 13:11
            b) Ephesians 4:3
        2. The things that build up others

Review

In his epistle to the Romans, Paul deals with the subject of salvation by grace through faith. Having laid out all the elements of salvation in the first eleven chapters, he teaches about the practical ramifications of that doctrine beginning in chapter 12. We all know that sin can be a blight on the fellowship of the redeemed, and Paul treats that subject in chapters 12 and 13. But another potential problem within the assembly is the conflict between strong and weak Christians. The strong understand their liberty—they can enjoy all the good things God has provided for them. But the weak can't understand their freedom—they remain restricted by non-moral taboos, traditions, and habits from their past life-style.

Christians are free to enjoy many things provided we do not use them to excess. Some of us understand that; some of us do not. So there exists the potential for conflict in the church over these things. Paul sets out to help us resolve that conflict in Romans 14:1–15:13.

The basic truth of Christian liberty is that we are free from the outward requirements of the Old Testament ceremonial laws. We are free to enjoy all of God's good gifts. However, we are never free to sin. Not all believers can accept that they are free to enjoy all God has provided. While the strong might feel they need to exercise their liberty, in so doing they greatly offend the weak and create conflict in the church. That ultimately disrupts the unity of the church and harms its testimony. Paul divided his discussion into four sections. We are looking at the second section, which is building up one another without offending (Rom. 14:13-23). To build up one another effectively, we must be willing to limit our liberty for the sake of a weaker believer. There are six ways to do that.

I. DON'T CAUSE YOUR BROTHER TO STUMBLE (v. 13; see pp. 51-54)

"Let us not, therefore, judge one another any more; but judge this, rather: that no man put a stumbling block or an occasion to fall in his brother's way."

II. DON'T GRIEVE YOUR BROTHER (vv. 14-15a; see pp. 54-57)

"I know, and am persuaded by the Lord Jesus, that there is nothing unclean of itself; but to him that esteemeth anything to be unclean, to him it is unclean. But if thy brother be grieved with thy food, now walkest thou not in love."

III. DON'T DEVASTATE YOUR BROTHER (v. 15b; see pp. 57-60)

"Destroy not him with thy food, for whom Christ died."

A. The Concept of Destruction (see pp. 57-59)

B. The Cause of Destruction (see p. 59)

C. The Contrast of Destruction (see pp. 59-60)

We are not to devastate fellow believers by plunging them into deep spiritual loss, possibly back into the milieu of pagan worship.

Lesson

Limited Atonement Versus Unlimited Atonement

The phrase at the end of Romans 14:15 says, "for whom Christ died." It is a key phrase that brings up the issue of atonement.

1. The perspective

   a) Limited atonement

   Some believe the phrase "for whom Christ died" proves that Christ died only for the elect—only for those who believe. That view is characteristic of historic Calvinists. Many Scripture verses teach that Christ did die specifically for believers. Here are a few.

   (1) Matthew 1:21—An angel said, "She shall bring forth a son, and thou shalt call his name Jesus; for he shall save his people from their sins."

   (2) John 10:15—Jesus said, "As the Father knoweth me, even so know I the Father; and I lay down my life for the sheep." Did Christ die only for the sheep? That verse implies He did.

   (3) Galatians 1:4—Paul says of the Lord Jesus Christ: "[He] gave himself for our sins, that he might deliver us from this present evil age." The word *us* refers to believers.

   (4) Ephesians 5:2—Paul said, "Walk in love, as Christ also hath loved us, and hath given himself for us an offering and a sacrifice to God."

   (5) Ephesians 5:25—Paul said, "Husbands, love your wives, even as Christ also loved the church, and gave himself for it."

   All those Scripture verses specifically say that Christ died for believers—for the elect. That is what theologians have called "particular redemption." They claim Christ did not die for the whole world—He died only for those who are or who will be redeemed. They fear that if Christ died for the whole world, but the whole world doesn't believe, then Christ died in futility. So to save Christ from a futile act, they particularize redemption.

   b) Unlimited atonement

   Here are some verses that give a different perspective.

(1) John 1:29—"The next day John [the Baptist] seeth Jesus coming unto him, and saith, Behold the Lamb of God, who taketh away the sin of the world."

(2) John 3:15-17—John the Baptist said of Jesus, "Whosoever believeth in him should not perish, but have eternal life. For God so loved the world, that he gave his only begotten Son, that whosoever believeth in him should not perish, but have everlasting life. For God sent not his Son into the world to condemn the world, but that the world through him might be saved."

(3) John 6:51—Jesus said, "I am the living bread that came down from heaven; if any man eat of this bread, he shall live forever; and the bread that I will give is my flesh, which I will give for the life of the world."

(4) Romans 10:13—Paul said, "Whosoever shall call upon the name of the Lord shall be saved."

(5) 2 Corinthians 5:14—Paul wrote, "The love of Christ constraineth us, because we thus judge that, if one died for all, then were all dead." The parallelism is inescapable. The reverse is: since all are dead in sin, therefore Christ died for all.

(6) 1 Timothy 2:3-4—Paul said, "God, our Savior . . . will have all men to be saved, and to come unto the knowledge of the truth."

(7) 1 Timothy 4:10—"Therefore, we both labor and suffer reproach, because we trust in the living God, who is the Savior of all men, specially of those that believe."

(8) 2 Peter 2:1—"There were false prophets also among the people, even as there shall be false teachers among you, who secretly shall bring in destructive heresies, even denying the Lord that bought them." The Lord paid the penalty for the sin of even the heretic, the apostate, the false teacher, and the unbeliever.

(9) 1 John 2:2—John tells us that Christ "is the propitiation [covering] for our sins, and not for ours only, but also for the sins of the whole world."

(10) 1 John 4:14—John said, "We have seen and do testify that the Father sent the Son to be the Savior of the world."

Those passages leave no doubt that Christ died for all mankind. Certainly there are passages that say Jesus died for the elect, but we can't conclude from them alone that He didn't die for the rest. I can say that Christ died on the cross for John MacArthur, but that is not necessarily an exclusive statement. Any verse that particularizes redemption to believers does not exclude that He died for the world as well.

2. The parallel

In the Old Covenant, the high point of the Jewish calendar each year was the Day of Atonement. On that day the sins of the nation were atoned for. Leviticus 16:15-17 says that the high priest was to "kill the goat of the sin offering, that is for the people, and bring its blood within the veil, and do with that blood as he did with the blood of the bullock, and sprinkle it upon the mercy seat, and before the mercy seat. And he shall make an atonement for the holy place, because of the uncleanness of the children of Israel, and because of their transgression in all their sins; and so shall he do for the tabernacle of the congregation, that remaineth among them in the midst of their uncleanness. And there shall be no man in the tabernacle of the congregation when he goeth in to make an atonement in the holy place, until he come out, and have made an atonement for himself, and for his household, and for all the congregation of Israel."

Verse 30 says, "On that day shall the priest make an atonement for you, to cleanse you, that you may be clean from all your sins before the Lord." Verses 33-34 conclude, "He shall make an atonement for the holy sanctuary, and he shall make an atonement for the tabernacle of the congregation, and for the altar; and he shall make an atonement for the priest, and for all the people of the congregation. And this shall be an everlasting statute unto you, to make an atonement for the children of Israel for all their sins once a year."

Was that a limited or unlimited atonement? It was unlimited. That atonement made for the whole nation did not necessarily guarantee the individual salvation of everyone in the nation—salvation then as now had to be personally appropriated. The

Day of Atonement in the Old Testament is the perfect parallel to the atonement of Christ in the New Testament. The former required an animal sacrifice; the latter involved the one perfect offering of Jesus Christ. He provides a universal redemption that is particularized only by those who put their faith in Him.

When we read Romans 14:15 and realize that the weak believer is devastated by our exercise of liberty and our failure to love him, we are reminded that he was one for whom Christ died. We are to build up our brother in love by not causing him to stumble, grieve, or be devastated by falling into sin.

IV. DON'T FORFEIT YOUR WITNESS (vv. 16-19)

A. The Christian Purpose (vv. 16-18)

"Let not then your good be evil spoken of; for the kingdom of God is not food and drink, but righteousness, and peace, and joy in the Holy Spirit. For he that in these things serveth Christ is acceptable to God, and approved of men."

It is possible to so abuse our liberty and create conflict with our weaker brothers that the world is turned off to Christianity because of how we treat one another. Instead of the world's seeing Christians as an admirable group of people, they disapprove of the conflict they see. Verse 18 says the church is to be "approved of men," a reference to people in general, not just to believers. The world is watching us, and it is important that we set aside our liberties for their sake, too.

First Peter 2:15 says, "So is the will of God, that with well doing [goodness of life and character] ye may put to silence the ignorance of foolish men." That means you shut the mouths of those who criticize your faith. How do you do that? Verse 16 says, "As free, and not using your liberty for a cloak of maliciousness." If you want to silence the critics by your good life, you can't abuse your freedom, and you certainly can't use your freedom as an excuse to cover your sin.

1. An authentic love (v. 16)

"Let not then your good be evil spoken of."

a) A blasphemous problem

What does "your good" refer to? The Greek word translated "good" is *agathos*. It refers to that which is qualitatively or intrinsically good. Paul has in mind our freedom in Christ—all that salvation provides, all the goodness of enjoying everything God has given us. When someone speaks evil about that good, it has just been blasphemed.

We can enjoy everything God has given us. A strong Christian can give thanks for his freedom and rejoice in it. But if he damages other people by abusing it, and the world sees his indifference to the pain of his weaker brother, do you think they will conclude that Christians are a marvelous group of people? Not at all. In Romans 2 Paul tells us that while the Jews were trying to show the world how righteous they were, they destroyed the reputation of God. In verse 24 he says, "The name of God is blasphemed among the Gentiles through you."

b) A scriptural principle

In 1 Corinthians 10:28-30 the apostle Paul says, "If any man say unto you, This is offered in sacrifice unto idols, eat not for his sake that showed it, and for conscience' sake; for the earth is the Lord's, and the fullness thereof—conscience, I say, not thine own, but of the other; for why is my liberty judged by another man's conscience? For if I, by grace, be a partaker, why am I evil spoken of for that for which I give thanks?"

This is what Paul means: Suppose you go to dinner at a pagan's house with another believer. Your host serves meat offered to idols. You're strong in the faith, but your fellow believer is weak. And you're both trying to evangelize the pagan. Your weaker brother puts an elbow in your ribs and whispers, "I can't eat that; it's meat offered to idols. My conscience won't allow me to eat it." But your host is proud of the fact that he is serving you meat sacrificed to idols. What are you going to do? Offend the pagan or the weaker believer? Offend the pagan. If you offend the weaker believer, you've discredited the significance of Christian love. If you offend the pagan to show love to a fellow believer, you've provided a profound testimony for that pagan. You have shown him that love overrules everything. That's the kind of fellowship most pagans would like to get into: a brotherhood where people care enough about each other to set aside their liberties. Perhaps the pagan will be drawn to the gospel by that example.

The point of Romans 14:16 is not to forfeit your witness by overdoing your liberty and offending a believer before an unbeliever. The unbeliever needs to see your love for your fellow believer. We don't need to show the world how free we are; we need to show how loving we are.

2. An appealing kingdom (v. 17)

   a) The non-essentials (v. 17a)

   "The kingdom of God is not food and drink."

   The kingdom is the sphere of salvation; it is God ruling in the hearts of those who believe in Christ. We all belong to it when we're saved. The essence of that kingdom is not meat and drink. We haven't been saved to promote externals or fight over non-essentials—though sad to say we've done it. I believe fighting over non-essentials has become widespread Christian recreation and is probably a key reason that many people reject the gospel. That's sad, because believers who fight over those things have missed the point of the kingdom.

   b) The necessary elements (v. 17b)

   "The kingdom of God is . . . righteousness, and peace, and joy in the Holy Spirit."

That is a comprehensive summary of the Christian life.

(1) Righteousness

The issue of the kingdom is righteous living—holy, obedient, God-honoring lives conformed to God's will. My chief concern is not liberty but holiness. That's what the watching world is looking for. I want to be filled with the fruits of righteousness and wear the breastplate of righteousness.

(2) Peace

The kingdom is all about having tranquil relationships with God and your fellow man. Our peace is exemplified by our caring and our unity. The tranquillity of our relationships can have a profound testimony. When the fruit of the Spirit (Gal. 5:22-23)—including love, joy, and peace—is displayed in our lives, the world sees Christianity as something desirable. Righteousness means I seek to honor God; peace means I seek to have harmony with my fellow believer.

(3) Joy

Someone who is right with God and at peace with his fellow believer will have joy. It's the personal joy of knowing God and experiencing forgiveness, grace, mercy, and love. It's the happy life of salvation that rejoices in everything.

We want the world to see Christians as those who are righteous, at peace, and filled with joy. And we will be that way when we exercise self-sacrificial love at the expense of exercising our liberties. The strong must move down to the level of weak believers and respect their weaknesses until they can be nurtured into strengths. There are things we are perfectly free to do that we must choose not to do to demonstrate to the watching world that the kingdom is not a celebration of our rights. When the world sees lives marked by righteousness—when it sees people with

integrity and honesty, who are just and virtuous—
that is a clear testimony to the reality of Christianity.
Even in the sinfulness of man there is enough of the
residual image of God for the unregenerate to long
for what is unobtainable to them. Peaceful relationships are foreign to the world because the world is
full of chaos. When the world sees deep, profound
joy in the Holy Spirit, it sees the heart of kingdom living. Those attractive elements can bring people to
Christ.

3. An acceptable servant (v. 18)

"He that in these things serveth Christ is acceptable to
God, and approved of men."

a) To God

Romans 12:1-2 says, "Present your bodies a living
sacrifice, holy, acceptable unto God, which is your
reasonable service. And be not conformed to this
world, but be ye transformed by the renewing of
your mind, that ye may prove what is that good, and
acceptable, and perfect, will of God." One who serves
Christ with righteousness, peace, and joy in the Holy
Spirit is pleasing to God.

b) To men

The true servant is also approved by men. In Titus
2:10 Paul says we should "adorn the doctrine of God."
We are to live lives that make God and His gospel attractive. Titus 2:5 speaks about women being "dis-
creet, chaste, keepers at home, good, obedient to
their own husbands, that the word of God be not
blasphemed." How we live together in righteousness, peace, and joy in the Holy Spirit is essential to
our testimony.

The Greek word translated "approve" in Romans
14:18 is *dokimos*, which means "to be approved after
close examination." We are under the scrutiny of the
world, and the world needs to see our love. We don't

want to cause another to stumble, grieve, or be devastated and end up forfeiting our witness.

In 1 Corinthians 9:1 the apostle Paul says, "Am I not an apostle, am I not free?" He had every right to do as he pleased in areas that were not sin. In verses 4-5 he says, "Have we no right to eat and to drink? Have we no right to lead about a sister, a wife?" Paul had every right to get married. In verses 6-7 he says, "Have we no right to forbear working? Who goeth to war at any time at his own expense? Who planteth a vineyard, and eateth not of its fruit? Or who feedeth a flock, and eateth not of the milk of the flock?" In verses 8-14 Paul continues to discuss his rights. Then in verse 15 he says, "I have used none of these things." Paul set aside all his rights because he didn't want to offend unbelievers.

In verses 19-22 he says, "Though I am free from all men, yet have I made myself servant unto all, that I might gain the more. And unto the Jews I became as a Jew, that I might gain the Jews; to them that are under the law, as under the law, not being myself under the law, that I might gain them that are under the law; to them that are without law, as without law (being not without law to God, but under the law to Christ), that I might gain them that are without law. To the weak became I as weak, that I might gain the weak; I am made all things to all men, that I might by all means save some." We should never reach the point where the exercise of our liberties causes us to be unconcerned about whether we might be offending the lost. In verse 23 Paul says, "And this I do for the gospel's sake." The ultimate freedom is to have freedom yet choose not to use it for the sake of others.

B. The Christian Pursuit (v. 19)

"Let us, therefore, follow after the things which make for peace, and things with which one may edify another."

We are to follow after (Gk., *diōkō*, "pursue") two things.

1. The things that make for peace

   Humility produces peace because someone with humility doesn't care about his own rights; he is more concerned about another's rights. Meekness, unselfishness, and love are the things that make for peace.

   a) 2 Corinthians 13:11—Paul said, "Finally, brethren, farewell. Be perfect, be of good comfort, be of one mind, live in peace."

   b) Ephesians 4:3—Paul said we're to be "endeavoring to keep the unity of the Spirit in the bond of peace."

   Peace is part of our testimony, so let's learn to pursue the things that make for peace. If you find a weaker brother in the fellowship who doesn't understand his liberty, reach down to where he is and make peace with him. Don't flaunt your liberty, especially knowing that unbelievers are watching you.

2. The things that build up others

   We should pursue the kinds of things that will bring about spiritual strengthening in a brother. In 1 Corinthians 14:12 Paul says, "Forasmuch as ye are zealous of spiritual gifts, seek that ye may excel to the edifying of the church." Seek the things that will build up your weaker brother, not that which will cause him to stumble, grieve, and be devastated.

V. DON'T TEAR DOWN THE WORK OF GOD (vv. 20-21)

   A. The General Command (v. 20)

      1. Examined (v. 20a)

         "For food destroy not the work of God."

         Paul has in mind the idea of offending a Jew with food that wasn't kosher or of offending a Gentile with food that had been offered to idols. But "food" is symbolic of any discretionary thing you might have a right to do.

We are not to destroy the work of God over discretionary things.

Verse 20 tells us that a weak believer is a work of God. Ephesians 2:10 says, "We are his workmanship, created in Christ Jesus." God is at work in every Christian, even the weaker brother. We are not to pull down what God is building up. Some people are so proud about their liberation that they don't care if they tear down a weaker believer.

The present imperative is used in Romans 14:20 for "destroy not." Paul is saying to stop what you're doing. Within that Roman assembly there must have been some liberated brethren who were tearing down what God was trying to build up. So Paul tells them to stop. They were not merely dealing with a man, but a man for whom Christ died—a man who was part of the kingdom and who had the Holy Spirit indwelling him. Now Paul adds that he also is a work of God. Would you take a black marker and scribble on the masterpieces in a museum? Would you cut through a Rembrandt with a knife? If you wouldn't do those things, then why would you tear down the work of the ultimate Master?

2. Explained (v. 20b)

"All things indeed are pure; but it is evil for that man who eateth with offense."

One who exercises his freedom at the expense of his brother is doing evil, even though the thing he is free to do isn't wrong in and of itself. All things are pure, but they become evil when they cause a brother to stumble, be grieved, or be devastated. That's why Paul says, "If food make my brother to offend, I will eat no meat" (1 Cor. 8:13).

B. The Specific Instruction (v. 21)

"It is good neither to eat meat, nor to drink wine, nor anything by which thy brother stumbleth, or is offended, or is made weak."

Drinking wine is not a moral evil; however, drunkenness is a sin. Drinking wine is not a sin if it does not contribute to losing your senses. The wine consumed in Paul's day was invariably mixed with water to avoid drunkenness. The fruit of the grape fermented and mixed with water in and of itself isn't wrong, but anything that causes your brother to stumble is wrong. If drinking wine causes your brother to stumble by tempting him to sin, it then is wrong. That is the primary reason I don't do many things I could, including drinking alcoholic beverages. I know some believers would be offended by it. If I were to drink wine, some would look down on me and deny me any godly virtue. But I joyously set such things aside because the greater issue is righteousness, peace, and joy in the Holy Spirit. Wine, food, cards, TV, and recreation are only things. It is how we use those things that matters. Sadly, many Christians will drink alcohol and flaunt their liberty no matter what anyone thinks. Consequently, there is a rift in the fellowship.

VI. DON'T FLAUNT YOUR LIBERTY (vv. 22-23)

A. A Word for the Strong Believer (v. 22)

"Hast thou faith? Have it to thyself before God. Happy is he that condemneth not himself in that thing which he alloweth."

According to Paul, the one who has faith is a strong believer—one who believes he has legitimate freedoms. If he understands his liberty then he should enjoy it before God. The person who does not condemn himself in what he approves is happy. He can enjoy his freedom and not feel self-condemned because he doesn't have a guilty conscience and he hasn't caused a believer to stumble. He can fully enjoy his freedom before the Lord.

B. A Word for the Weak Believer (v. 23)

"He that doubteth is condemned if he eat, because he eateth not of faith; for whatever is not of faith is sin."

The weak Christian shouldn't try to emulate the strong until he believes an action is right. Otherwise, he will be condemned by his conscience.

How can the strong Christian be happy? By setting aside his liberty and enjoying it only before the Lord. He will be happy because he won't be condemning himself for the things he is doing that cause problems for others. The weak believer will be happy when he doesn't participate in things he isn't ready to handle. If he does he will go against his conscience, and that will be sin to him. It will result in guilt and a loss of joy. Don't flaunt your freedom; enjoy it before the Lord.

Conclusion

To maintain unity in the church we are to receive one another and build up one another without offending. Paul sums it up in 1 Corinthians 10:31-33: "Whether, therefore, ye eat, or drink, or whatever ye do, do all to the glory of God. Give no offense, neither to the [unsaved] Jews, nor to the Greeks [unsaved Gentiles], nor to the church of God; even as I please all men in all things, not seeking mine own profit, but the profit of many, that they may be saved." The ultimate goal of unity between strong and weak believers is a profound testimony to the world that brings about the salvation of many.

Focusing on the Facts

1. What is limited atonement? What Scripture verses support that position? What is unlimited atonement? What Scripture verses support that position (see pp. 47-50)?
2. What Old Testament event provides a parallel to unlimited atonement (see p. 50)?
3. What can cause people in the world to disapprove of Christians (see p. 51)?
4. How can Christians silence the critics of the world (1 Peter 2:15-16; see p. 51)?
5. When you find yourself in a situation where you have to offend either a believer or an unbeliever, whom should you offend? Why (see pp. 52-53)?

6. What three elements characterize the kingdom of God? Explain each (Rom. 14:17; see pp. 53-54).
7. What will attract the unsaved to Christianity (see pp. 54-55)?
8. From whom does the Christian gain approval when he limits his liberty for the sake of a weaker believer (Rom. 14:18; see p. 55)?
9. According to 1 Corinthians 9:23, what was Paul's reason for limiting his liberty (see p. 56)?
10. What two things should a believer pursue? Explain (Rom. 14:19; see pp. 56-57).
11. What does the word *food* represent in Romans 14:20 (see p. 57)?
12. What does the phrase "work of God" refer to in Romans 14:20 (see p. 58)?
13. When do things that are pure become evil (Rom. 14:21; see p. 59)?
14. What concluding words does Paul have for the strong? for the weak (Rom. 14:22-23; see pp. 59-60)?
15. What is the ultimate goal of unity between strong and weak Christians (see p. 60)?

Pondering the Principles

1. Many passages of Scripture show us that Christ died for the world. Review the verses on pages 49-50. Knowing that God wants all men to be saved, what changes do you need to make in your commitment to evangelize the unsaved? Ask God to help you acquire the right attitude toward unbelievers. Look up the following verses: Matthew 9:36-38, 18:11-13, and 2 Corinthians 8:9. What kind of attitude did Christ display toward the unsaved? Seek to be like the Lord, especially in His attitude toward the lost.

2. Put yourself in the place of your unsaved relatives or neighbors. What can they conclude about Christianity based on what they see in your relationships with other Christians? Are there aspects of those relationships that might lead them to think less of Christianity? What changes can you make to improve your testimony to your unsaved relatives and neighbors? What liberties do you need to give up to demonstrate love to your weaker brothers? Memorize Romans 14:16 as a constant reminder against abusing your liberty before a watching world: "Do not let what is for you a good thing be spoken of as evil" (NASB).

3. On a scale of 1-10, rate yourself in your practice of righteousness, peace, and joy. Which one is your strength? Which one is your weakness? How do you think the unsaved people you know would rate you in each of those areas? Which one would they classify as your weakness? Make it your goal this week to improve your weaknesses. Look for places where you need to be more obedient. At every opportunity strive to be at peace with all your fellow believers. See if your joy doesn't improve when you become more obedient to God and develop peace with your brothers and sisters in Christ.

5

Pleasing One Another
for the Sake of Christ

Outline

Introduction
A. God's Concern for Unity
   1. The concern of God the Father
      a) His design for Israel
         (1) Ezekiel 37:16-17
         (2) Zephaniah 3:9
         (3) Zechariah 14:9
         (4) Hosea 1:11
      b) His design for the church
   2. The concern of God the Son
   3. The concern of God the Holy Spirit
      a) Acts 2:38, 41-46
      b) Acts 4:31-32
B. Scripture's Emphasis on Unity

Lesson
I. Consideration of Others (v. 1*a*)
  A. Showing Patience to the Weaker Brother
  B. Owing a Debt to the Weaker Brother
    1. Bearing the weak
      a) 1 Corinthians 9:19, 22
      b) Romans 13:8
    2. Pleasing the weak
II. Disregard for Self (vv. 1*b*-2)
  A. Making a Sacrifice for the Weaker Brother (v. 1*b*)
  B. Helping to Strengthen the Weaker Brother (v. 2)
    1. 1 Corinthians 10:23-24
    2. Philippians 2:1-3, 5-8

Introduction

A. God's Concern for Unity

Discord strikes a deadly blow at God's work in the church. Chaos, strife, envy, anger, bitterness, dissension, and self-ishness violate the unity of the church. They violate the will of God and cripple His testimony in the world. The harmony of the church is of grave concern to God.

1. The concern of God the Father

Psalm 133:1-3 says, "Behold, how good and how pleas-ant it is for brethren to dwell together in unity! It is like the precious ointment upon the head, that ran down upon the beard, even Aaron's beard; that went down to the skirts of his garments. Like the dew of Hermon, and like the dew that descended upon the mountains of Zion, for there the Lord commanded the blessing, even life for evermore." Unity is a sweet and fragrant offering to God.

In Jeremiah 32:38-39 God says the following concerning those who would some day become partakers of the New Covenant: "They shall be my people, and I will be their God. And I will give them one heart, and one way, that they may fear me forever, for the good of them, and of their children after them."

a) His design for Israel

   (1) Ezekiel 37:16-17—The chapter begins with a vision of a valley of dry bones, which is a picture of God's regathering of the nation of Israel. But as the Lord looks ahead to the future glory of His redeemed nation, he says, "Moreover, thou son of man, take thee one stick, and write upon it, For Judah, and for the children of Israel, his companions; then take another stick, and write upon it, For Joseph, the stick of Ephraim, and for all the house of Israel, his companions; and join them one to another into one stick, and they shall become one in thy hand." Those two sticks represent the divided kingdom under Rehoboam and Jeroboam. Judah represents the Southern Kingdom and Joseph the Northern Kingdom. One day God will join together a divided kingdom in final glory.

   Using sticks as symbols for the kingdoms would not have been foreign to Ezekiel's audience. Numbers 17:2 says every tribe had a stick to identify it.

   (2) Zephaniah 3:9—The Lord said, "Then will I turn to the peoples a pure language, that they may all call upon the name of the Lord, to serve him with one consent."

   (3) Zechariah 14:9—Zechariah wrote, "The Lord shall be king over all the earth; in that day shall there be one Lord, and his name one." All the inhabitants of the earth will hold up the name of the Lord and exalt Him.

(4) Hosea 1:11—The Lord said, "Then shall the children of Judah and the children of Israel be gathered together, and appoint themselves one head, and they shall come up out of the land, for great shall be the day of Jezreel."

God has long intended through the New Covenant to bring the nation of Israel together as one people.

b) His design for the church

Just as all the rebels will be purged out from the nation of Israel in the future so that it may be one, so it is in the church. In John 10:14-17 Jesus says, "I am the good shepherd, and know my sheep, and am known of mine. As the Father knoweth me, even so I know the Father; and I lay down my life for the sheep. And other sheep I have, that are not of this fold [Gentiles]; them also I must bring, and they shall hear my voice; and there shall be one fold, and one shepherd. Therefore doth my Father love me, because I lay down my life, that I might take it again." It was God's purpose for Christ to lay down His life to redeem both Jew and Gentile and make them one people.

God's desire is to make the nation of Israel one. It is also His desire to blend together the redeemed nation and the redeemed church. That's reflected in 1 Corinthians 15:28: "When all things shall be subdued unto him [Christ], then shall the Son also himself be subject unto him that put all things under him, that God may be all in all."

God's desire is for all His people to be one, with one heart and one voice. The unity of the redeemed is the purpose of God, and that purpose ultimately finds its outworking in eternal glory. Revelation 21:2-4 says, "I, John, saw the holy city, new Jerusalem, coming down from God out of heaven, prepared as a bride adorned for her husband. And I heard a great voice out of heaven saying, Behold, the tabernacle of God is with men, and he will dwell with them, and they shall be his people, and God himself shall be with them, and be their

God. And God shall wipe away all tears from their eyes; and there shall be no more death, neither sorrow, nor crying, neither shall there be any more pain; for the former things are passed away." All redeemed people will be brought together with God as their King.

2. The concern of God the Son

In John 17:11 Jesus prays to the Father, "Now I am no more in the world, but these are in the world, and I come to thee. Holy Father, keep through thine own name those whom thou hast given me, that they may be one, as we are." In verse 20 He says, "Neither pray I for these alone, but for them also who shall believe on me through their word." Jesus prayed not only for His disciples but also for all who would believe in the future. The content of His prayer is: "That they all may be one, as thou, Father, art in me, and I in thee, that they also may be one in us; that the world may believe that thou hast sent me. And the glory which thou gavest me I have given them, that they may be one, even as we are one" (vv. 21-22). It is the particular concern of God the Son that we be one.

3. The concern of God the Holy Spirit

In Acts 2:4 the believers were all filled with the Holy Spirit. As a result, some wonderful things happened.

a) Acts 2:38, 41-46—Peter said, "Repent, and be baptized, every one of you, in the name of Jesus Christ for the remission of sins, and ye shall receive the gift of the Holy Spirit" (v. 38). What was the result? Verses 41-46 say, "They that gladly received his word were baptized; and the same day there were added unto them about three thousand souls. And they continued steadfastly in the apostles' doctrine and fellowship, and in breaking of bread, and in prayers. And fear came upon every soul; and many wonders and signs were done by the apostles. And all that believed were together, and had all things common; and sold their possessions and goods, and parted them to all men, as every man had need. And they, continuing daily with one accord in the temple, and breaking bread from house to house, did eat their food with gladness and singleness of heart." The first characteristic of the redeemed was a unity of spirit. They were of one accord—one in praise, fellowship, breaking of bread, prayer, doctrine, proclamation, and sharing their goods. That was the result of God's Spirit within them.

b) Acts 4:31-32—When the church had prayed, "the place was shaken where they were assembled together; and they were all filled with the Holy Spirit, and they spoke the word of God with boldness. And the multitude of those that believed were of one heart and of one soul." The people responded as one when they were filled with the Holy Spirit.

It is the desire of God the Father, God the Son, and God the Holy Spirit that we be one. We are to be one not only in terms of our position but also in practice by sharing in our fellowship. Ephesians 4:3-6 gives us the details. Verse 3 says we're to be "endeavoring to keep the unity of the Spirit in the bond of peace." One of the primary tasks of the church is to maintain our unity, and that unity is reinforced by the Trinity. Verse 4 talks about the Spirit: "There is one body, and one Spirit, even as ye are called in one hope of your calling." Verse 5 talks about the Son: "[There is] one Lord, one faith, one baptism." And verse 6 talks about the Father: "[There is] one God and Father of all, who is above all, and through all, and in you all."

B. Scripture's Emphasis on Unity

Since unity is the will of the Trinity, we find it constantly emphasized in the New Testament.

1. 1 Corinthians 1:10—"I beseech you, brethren, by the name of our Lord Jesus Christ, that ye all speak the same thing, and that there be no divisions among you, but that ye be perfectly joined together in the same mind and in the same judgment."

2. 1 Corinthians 3:1-3—"I, brethren, could not speak unto you as unto spiritual, but as unto carnal, even as unto babes in Christ. I have fed you with milk, and not with

solid food; for to this time ye were not able to bear it, neither yet now are ye able. For ye are yet carnal; for there is among you envying, and strife, and divisions, are ye not carnal, and walk as men?"

3. 1 Corinthians 12:12-14—"As the body is one, and hath many members, and all the members of that one body, being many, are one body, so also is Christ. For by one Spirit were we all baptized into one body, whether we be Jews or Greeks, whether we be bond or free; and have been all made to drink into one Spirit. For the body is not one member, but many."

4. Galatians 3:26-28—"Ye are all the sons of God by faith in Christ Jesus. For as many of you as have been baptized into Christ have put on Christ. There is neither Jew nor Greek, there is neither bond nor free, there is neither male nor female; for ye are all one in Christ Jesus."

5. Philippians 1:27—"Let your conduct be as it becometh the gospel of Christ, that whether I come and see you, or else be absent, I may hear of your affairs, that ye stand fast in one spirit, with one mind striving together for the faith of the gospel."

6. Philippians 2:2—"Fulfill ye my joy, that ye be like-minded, having the same love, being of one accord, of one mind."

7. Colossians 3:11, 14-15—"There is neither Greek nor Jew, circumcision nor uncircumcision, barbarian, Scythian, bond nor free, but Christ is all, and in all. . . . Put on love, which is the bond of perfectness. And let the peace of God rule in your hearts, to which also ye are called in one body."

8. 1 Peter 3:8-9—"Be ye all of one mind, having compassion one of another, love as brethren, be pitiful, be courteous, not rendering evil for evil, or railing for railing, but on the contrary, blessing, knowing that ye are called to this, that ye should inherit a blessing."

9. 2 John 4—"I rejoiced greatly that I found of thy children walking in truth."

10. 3 John 2, 4—"I wish above all things that thou mayest prosper and be in health. . . . I have no greater joy than to hear that my children walk in truth."

Paul realized that one of the great dangers to unity in the church is the potential discord between strong and weak Christians. Since unity is so important to God, Paul found it essential to teach about it in Romans 14:1–15:13. In this lesson we will examine Romans 15:1-7: "We, then, that are strong ought to bear the infirmities of the weak, and not to please ourselves. Let every one of us please his neighbor for his good to edification. For even Christ pleased not himself; but, as it is written, The reproaches of them that reproached thee fell on me. For whatever things were written in earlier times were written for our learning, that we, through patience and comfort of the scriptures, might have hope. Now the God of patience and consolation grant you to be likeminded one toward another according to Christ Jesus, that ye may with one mind and one mouth glorify God, even the Father of our Lord Jesus Christ. Wherefore, receive ye one another, as Christ also received us to the glory of God."

Throughout Romans 14:1–15:13 Paul emphasizes four major principles that must govern the relationship of strong and weak Christians. We are looking at the third one: pleasing one another for the sake of Christ We have to be concerned with pleasing others, not ourselves, to make unity a reality. That's following our Lord's example. If everyone aims only to please himself, we will have chaos. It is incumbent on strong believers to please the weak. This text has six principles for the strong to consider.

Lesson

I. CONSIDERATION OF OTHERS (v. 1a)

"We, then, that are strong ought to bear the infirmities of the weak."

A. Showing Patience to the Weaker Brother

Being considerate of others is seeking to serve them with love rather than attack them with criticism. Paul encouraged the strong believer to set aside his liberty and lovingly bear with the weak. Some people are still bound to religious taboos from the past, and we need to be patient until they grow away from such things. Being considerate is the first attitude we must have before we can please someone else. Philippians 2:4 says, "Look not every man on his own things, but every man also on the things of others." We are to avoid things that might distress others. When someone struggles with some non-moral thing you believe is right but he believes is wrong, be patient with him until he understands his freedom in Christ.

B. Owing a Debt to the Weaker Brother

1. Bearing the weak

The Greek word translated "ought" in Romans 15:1 means "to be a debtor." Paul uses the same word in Romans 1:14: "I am debtor both to the Greeks and to the barbarians." Our debt is "to bear (Gk., *bastazō*) the infirmities of the weak." That word is used more than twenty-five times in the New Testament. It does not communicate the idea of tolerating someone's inadequacy; it refers to carrying someone's load—of shouldering his burden. Galatians 6:2 says, "Bear ye one another's burdens, and so fulfill the law of Christ." The same word is used in Mark 14:13 and Luke 22:10 of carrying a water pitcher. In Luke 7:14 it's used of carrying a stretcher, in John 10:31 of carrying stones, in John 12:6 of carrying a bag of money, in Acts 15:10 of carrying a yoke, in Acts 21:35 of carrying a man, and in Revelation 17:7 of carrying a woman. In Romans 15:1 Paul is urging the strong to come under the weak believer, to walk along with him in his weakness until he can grow to understand his freedom. We need to carry the errors of the weak by coming alongside of them and nurturing them in their walk.

a) 1 Corinthians 9:19, 22—Paul said, "I am free from all men, yet have I made myself servant unto all, that I might gain the more. . . . To the weak became I as weak, that I might gain the weak." Although the context is different from Romans 15:1, the principle is the same. If we're going to gain the weak, we need to get under their load and shoulder it with them.

b) Romans 13:8—Paul said, "Owe no man any thing, but to love one another." That's a debt we'll never fully pay off; we'll always owe it.

2. Pleasing the weak

Some people believe Paul is saying we ought to be men-pleasers. Galatians 1:10 defines a man-pleaser as one who adjusts the gospel to fit what people want and backs away from confronting sin. That's not what Paul is saying in Romans 15:1, nor is he saying we should be like Absalom, who was a man-pleaser for his own gain. Absalom was the son of David who wanted to dethrone his father. Second Samuel 15:2-3 says, "Absalom rose up early, and stood beside the way of the gate; and it was that, when any man who had a controversy came to the king for judgment, then Absalom called unto him, and said, Of what city art thou? And he said, Thy servant is one of the tribes of Israel. And Absalom said unto him, See, thy matters are good and right; but there is no man deputed of the king to hear thee."

As people came with grievances for the king, Absalom stopped them and sympathized with their plight. Then Absalom said, "Oh that I were made judge in the land, that every man who hath any suit or cause might come unto me, and I would do him justice! And it was that, when any man came near to him to do him obeisance, he put forth his hand, and took him, and kissed him. And on this manner did Absalom to all Israel that came to the king for judgment; so Absalom stole the hearts of the men of Israel" (vv. 4-6). Absalom had an ulterior motive. He was a man-pleaser for his own gains.

Paul is not telling us to please men by adjusting the gospel, ignoring sin, or attracting them to us for our own gain. He wants us to please those who need help in carrying the load of bondage they are not yet ready to give up. That's being considerate.

II. DISREGARD FOR SELF (vv. 1b-2)

A. Making a Sacrifice for the Weaker Brother (v. 1b)

"Not to please ourselves."

Our pleasure is not the criterion for what we can or cannot do. That is not a spiritual approach. In Philippians 2:19-21 Paul says, "I trust in the Lord Jesus to send Timothy shortly unto you. . . . For I have no man likeminded, who will naturally care for your state. For all seek their own, not the things which are Jesus Christ's." What a sad commentary! People in whom Paul had invested a great deal of time were now seeking to fulfill their own desires and not those of Christ. The idea behind Christian liberty is that although you are free to do many things, you avoid what might offend or cause another believer to stumble.

B. Helping to Strengthen the Weaker Brother (v. 2)

"Let every one of us please his neighbor for his good to edification."

No one gets off the hook—everyone is obligated to please his neighbor with the goal of building him up. In Romans 14:19 Paul says, "Let us, therefore, follow after the things which make for peace, and things with which one may edify another."

Strong believers are responsible for the spiritual growth of the weak. That is not to say they should sacrifice God's truth for the sake of harmony, but they should set aside their liberty with regard to neutral things for the purpose of building up the weak. When a strong believer flaunts his liberty, the weak are made weaker. To lift them from their weakness, the strong must be sure to do what pleases them.

1. 1 Corinthians 10:23-24—Paul said, "All things are lawful for me, but all things are not expedient; all things are

91

lawful for me, but all things edify not. Let no man seek his own, but every man another's wealth."

2. Philippians 2:1-3, 5-8—Paul said, "If there be, therefore, any consolation in Christ, if any comfort of love, if any fellowship of the Spirit, if any tender mercies and compassions, fulfill ye my joy, that ye be like-minded. . . . In lowliness of mind let each esteem others better than themselves. . . . Let this mind be in you, which was also in Christ Jesus, who, being in the form of God, thought it not robbery to be equal with God, but made himself of no reputation, and took upon him the form of a servant, and was made in the likeness of men; and, being found in fashion as a man, he humbled himself and became obedient unto death, even the death of the cross."

III. CONFORMITY TO CHRIST (v. 3)

"Even Christ pleased not himself; but, as it is written, the reproaches of them that reproached thee fell on me."

A. The Responsibility of Christ

Christ did not please Himself; He took the reproach of God. Christ suffered. If He had really wanted to please Himself, He would have remained in glory with God. In John 17:5 He says, "O Father, glorify thou me with thine own self with the glory which I had with thee before the world was."

1. To please the Father

   a) John 4:34—"Jesus saith unto [His disciples], My food is to do the will of him that sent me, and to finish his work."

   b) John 5:30—"I seek not mine own will, but the will of the Father who hath sent me."

   c) John 6:38—"I came down from heaven, not to do mine own will but the will of him that sent me."

d) John 8:25-29—The scribes and Pharisees said to Jesus, "Who art thou? And Jesus saith unto them, Even the same that I said unto you from the beginning. I have many things to say and to judge of you; but he that sent me is true; and I speak to the world those things which I have heard of him. They understood not that he spoke to them of the Father. Then said Jesus to them, When ye have lifted up the Son of man, then shall ye know that I am he, and that I do nothing of myself; but as my Father hath taught me, I speak these things. And he that sent me is with me. The Father hath not left me alone; for I do always those things that please him." Christ did the things that pleased the Father.

e) John 14:31—"That the world may know that I love the Father, and, as the Father gave me commandment, even so I do."

f) Hebrews 3:2—Christ Jesus "was faithful to him that appointed him."

g) Hebrews 5:7-8—Christ, "in the days of his flesh, when he had offered up prayers and supplications with strong crying and tears [in the garden of Gethsemane] unto him that was able to save him from death, and was heard in that he feared, though he were a Son, yet learned he obedience by the things which he suffered." Christ cried out to the Father for deliverance, but God chose not to deliver Him. And Christ was perfectly content to obey Him, saying, "Not my will, but thine, be done" (Luke 22:42).

Jesus came not to please Himself but to please the Father. He is our pattern.

2. To please the elect

In pleasing the Father, Jesus was also able to please and bless us (John 17:24-26). No one compelled Jesus to do what He did. In John 10:18 He says, "No man taketh [my life] from me, but I lay it down of myself. I have power to lay it down, and I have power to take it again."

Christians are to conform to Christ. That means we seek to be like Him rather than to make everyone be like us. And being like Him means we don't do what pleases us but what pleases others.

B. The Reproach of Christ

"The reproaches of them that reproached thee fell on me" (Rom. 15:3) comes from Psalm 69. Much of that psalm is about the Messiah and His agony. "They that hate me without a cause" (v. 4) speaks of men's hatred of the Lord. Verse 8 says, "I am become a stranger unto my brethren, and an alien unto my mother's children." That verse was fulfilled in John 1:11: "He came unto his own, and his own received him not." Psalm 69:14-20 may well refer to Christ's agony in the Garden of Gethsemane. "They gave me also gall for my food, and in my thirst they gave me vinegar to drink" (v. 21) refers to His crucifixion. But it is verse 9 that Paul quotes, which says, "The reproaches of those who reproached thee are fallen upon me." In pleasing the Father, Christ received reproach: slander, false accusations, and insults. Christ received all that because He represented God. Men hate God, and they hate the One who revealed Him. They hate the holiness of God, and they hate the holiness of Christ.

A willingness to please God in spite of inevitable reproach is a key Christian attitude. Christ was willing to endure anything for the sake of doing the Father's will. He was indifferent to His own deprivation and agony. His willingness to please the Father is our example. Rather than trying to please ourselves, we should follow Christ's pattern and be willing to suffer anything in pleasing another. He set aside all His divine rights to be subject to the Father and suffer for the sake of sinners. Can we do less for a fellow Christian? First John 2:6 says, "He that saith he abideth in him ought himself also so to walk, even as he walked."

IV. SUBMISSION TO SCRIPTURE (v. 4)

"Whatever things were written in earlier times were written for our learning, that we, through patience and comfort of the scriptures, might have hope."

We are to seek fulfillment in the Word of God, not from personal pursuits. We ought to conform to what the Word of God teaches.

A. The Value of Scripture

In his justification for using the Old Testament in verse 3, Paul affirms the value of Scripture in general. The phrase "whatever things were written in earlier times" refers to the Old Testament. Second Peter 1:21 says, "Holy men of God spoke as they were moved by the Holy Spirit." That verse also refers to the Old Testament. The phrase "was written for our learning" tells us that the Old Testament is not a dead book. First Corinthians 10:6, 11 tell us it provides us with examples. Paul said to Timothy, "All scripture is given by inspiration of God, and is profitable for doctrine, for reproof, for correction, for instruction in righteousness, that the man of God may be perfect, thoroughly furnished unto all good works" (2 Tim. 3:16-17).

B. The Instruction of Scripture

Scripture teaches us in Romans 15:4 that "we, through patience [Gk., *hupomonē*, "endurance"] and comfort [encouragement] of the scriptures, might have hope." I believe man needs hope more than anything else. The goal of Scripture is to give us hope—hope for the future, for eternal life, for forgiveness from sin, and for the meaning of life. In Jeremiah 14:8 God is called "the hope of Israel." He is the giver of hope. The author of Psalm 119 says, "I hope in thy Word" (vv. 81, 114).

Our hope is based on what the Bible reveals. Would you have hope in the life to come if you'd never read Scripture? No. That's why Ephesians 2:12 says that those without the Scriptures were without hope and without God in the world. Without the Word of God we have no basis for hope. We wouldn't know about heaven, about Christ and His kingdom, or about the glorious reward that lies ahead.

Scripture gives us hope, and it is realized through two great spiritual realities: endurance and encouragement.

1. Endurance

Scripture tells us we can endure any trial, difficulty, or anxiety. James 5:7-8 says, "Be patient therefore, brethren, unto the coming of the Lord. Behold, the farmer waiteth for the precious fruit of the earth, and hath long patience for it, until he receive the early and latter rain. Be ye also patient, establish your hearts; for the coming of the Lord draweth near." Endurance comes from confidence in Scripture. The Bible tells us we have the power to patiently endure this life, waiting for the hope that awaits us. We could not endure our trials if we had no word from God about the security of the believer. If we didn't know we were secure, every time trouble came we might think we were thrown out of God's kingdom. But Scripture tells us to endure, to be strengthened, and to develop patience so that we can be more useful to God and more effective in winning others (James 1:4).

2. Encouragement

The Greek word translated "comfort" in Romans 15:4 is *paraklēsis.* Another form is *paraklētos*—one who comes alongside to encourage. The Word of God not only tells us how to endure but also encourages us in the process.

We have hope, and that hope is anchored in the Word of God. We need to learn from Scripture. A biblical mind-set is the key ingredient for the strong believer's attitude toward a weaker brother. One aspect of learning patience and encouragement is learning to tolerate weaker brothers. Learn to wait for the day you can exercise your freedom before your weaker brother, and let God's Word encourage you while you endure.

V. DEPENDENCE ON DIVINE POWER (v. 5)

"Now the God of patience and consolation grant you to be like-minded one toward another according to Christ Jesus."

A. Praying for Strength

Paul realized the strong believer must depend on the power of God because he can't love his weaker brother on his own. If we depend on human resources we'll be impatient and weak. Through prayer we depend on God. The God of endurance and encouragement will allow us to endure deprivations of our liberty and encourage us in the process.

B. Praying for Unity

Paul prayed that God might lead all believers to be like-minded toward one another or to have the same concerns. The attitude of likemindedness reveals a loving concern that brings about unity. Paul is not referring to doctrinal unity. We assume there will be disagreement on minor doctrines. But in spite of that, there should be harmony in relationships. Where there is discord on doctrine regarding neutral things, then the strong need to come alongside the weak and bring unity despite differences of opinion. But only God can produce that ability in the strong believer. That's why the apostles gave themselves to prayer and the ministry of the Word (Acts 6:4). What about your prayer life? When did you last pray for the unity of the church? When did you last pray for God to make you one who could sustain the weak?

VI. GLORY TO GOD (vv. 6-7)

We should have a consuming desire for God to be glorified.

A. The Essence of Christ (v. 6)

"That ye may with one mind and one mouth glorify God, even the Father of our Lord Jesus Christ.

Every time Jesus spoke to God, He addressed Him as Father, except on the cross, where He said, "My God, My God, why hast thou forsaken me?" (Matt. 27:46). He also

97

instructed believers to address God as Father (Matt. 6:9). Paul, in describing God as the Father of our Lord Jesus Christ, is proclaiming the deity of Jesus Christ. John 5:17-18 says, "My Father worketh hitherto, and I work. Therefore, the Jews sought the more to kill him, because he . . . said also that God was his Father, making himself equal with God." Anytime the Bible refers to God as the Father of our Lord Jesus Christ, it emphasizes that God is one with Christ. Paul emphasized that many times:

1. Ephesians 1:3—"Blessed be the God and Father of our Lord Jesus Christ."

2. Ephesians 1:17—"The God of our Lord Jesus Christ, the Father of glory."

3. 2 Corinthians 1:3—"Blessed be God, even the Father of our Lord Jesus Christ."

God is the Father of the Lord Jesus Christ—God and Christ are one. Therefore no man can come to God except by Christ (John 14:6). No one worships God unless he recognizes Him as the Father of Christ (John 5:23).

Paul in Romans 15:6 instructs believers to maintain unity with one mind (internally) and one mouth (externally) for the purpose of glorifying God.

B. The Example of Christ (v. 7)

"Wherefore, receive ye one another, as Christ also received us to the glory of God."

Christ received us when we were vile, lost sinners to glorify God. As Christ thus received us, so we are to receive each other that we might glorify God.

A consideration of others, disregard for self, conformity to Christ, submission to Scripture, dependence on divine power, and a desire to glorify God are essential if we are to manifest, enjoy, and glorify God with unity in the church.

Focusing on the Facts

1. What things violate the unity of the church (see p. 82)?
2. What is God's desire for Israel and the church? Explain (see pp. 83-84).
3. Describe the unity displayed by members of the early church in Acts 2:41-46 (see pp. 85-86).
4. Explain how unity in the church is reinforced by the Trinity (Eph. 4:3-6; see p. 86).
5. Give some examples of how Scripture emphasizes unity (see pp. 86-88).
6. What does it mean to be considerate of others (see p. 89)?
7. What is Paul communicating by his use of the Greek word translated "bear" in Romans 15:1 (see p. 89)?
8. In what way was Absalom a man-pleaser (see p. 90)?
9. What criteria should we use for exercising our liberty in Christ (see p. 91)?
10. What responsibility do strong believers have toward the weak (Rom. 15:2; see p. 91)?
11. Whom did Christ please? Support your answer with Scripture (see pp. 92-94).
12. What did Christ receive as a result of His example (Ps. 69:9; see p. 94)?
13. How can we follow Christ's example in pleasing others (see p. 94)?
14. We should seek fulfillment from the _____ of _____, not from _____ _____ (see p. 95).
15. What is the value of Scripture (2 Tim. 3:16-17; see p. 95)?
16. According to Romans 15:4, what does Scripture teach us? Explain (see p. 95).
17. In what two ways does Scripture give us hope (see p. 96)?
18. What happens when believers depend on human resources? What happens when we depend on God's strength (see p. 97)?
19. What should be the consuming desire of all believers (see p. 97)?
20. How does Paul proclaim the deity of Christ in Romans 15:6 (see p. 98)?

1. Read the following verses: 1 Corinthians 1:10, Philippians 1:27, 2:2, Colossians 3:14-15, and 1 Peter 3:8-9. Make a list of the things you are responsible to do to help maintain unity in the church. Next to each item, indicate whether you are above average, average, or below average in your practice of maintaining unity. Isolate the one thing in which you believe you need the most improvement. Make it your goal this week to improve in that area.

2. According to Romans 15:1-2, the strong believers owe a debt to the weak: to shoulder their burdens and build them up spiritually. The only way to do that is to sacrifice our desires for their sake. Read Philippians 2:1-8. According to verses 1-4, what should our priority be? What can you practically apply from Christ's example in verses 5-8? How might you treat a weak believer by following Christ's example?

3. Do you pray for the unity of the church? How often? Based on what you have learned about the importance of unity, how often should you pray for that? Take this time to pray for the unity of the church as a whole and in particular for your local congregation. If you know people who aren't getting along, pray for them. Finally, pray for your specific role in helping to maintain unity. Ask God to give you opportunities to make sacrifices for others so that the church might be more unified.

6
Rejoicing with One Another in the Plan of God

Outline

Review

Lesson
I. The Basic Instruction (v. 7)
  A. The Intensity of the Command
    1. The illustrations
    2. The implications
      a) For the Gentile
      b) For the Jew
  B. The Pattern of the Command
    1. Christ's merciful standard
    2. Christians' merciless standard
  C. The Reason for the Command
    1. The purpose
    2. The pattern
      a) Christ receives sinners with joy
        (1) The illustration
        (2) The principle
        (3) The application
      b) Christ receives sinners despite their sin
        (1) The illustrations
          (*a*) Christ's relationship with sinners
          (*b*) Christ's reception of a sinner
        (2) The principle
      c) Christ receives sinners without partiality
      d) Christ receives sinners to glorify God

II. The Biblical Illustrations (vv. 8-12)
- A. The Proof of Equal Salvation (vv. 8-9*a*)
    1. Showing Jews the truth of God (v. 8)
        a) Jesus fulfilled prophecy
        b) Jesus verified God's truth
            (1) The testimony of Mary
            (2) The testimony of Zacharias
    2. Showing Gentiles the mercy of God (v. 9*a*)
- B. The Promise of Equal Salvation (vv. 9*b*-12)
    1. Psalm 18:49 (v. 9*b*)
    2. Deuteronomy 32:43 (v. 10)
    3. Psalm 117:1 (v. 11)
    4. Isaiah 11:1, 10 (v. 12)

III. The Benedictory Intercession (v. 13)

Review

In Romans 1:1-17 Paul gives a preview of his epistle by introducing his theme: the saving gospel of Jesus Christ. As Paul unfolds the gospel, he discusses sin in Romans 1:18–3:20. Then in Romans 3:21–11:36 he describes the implications of salvation from sin. He follows that with instructions in Romans 12:1–15:13 for practical Christian living in response to the saving work of Christ. In the last part of that section (14:1–15:13), Paul teaches about the relationship between strong and weak Christians. He gives four principles for governing their relationships. We will look at the fourth principle, which is rejoicing with one another in the plan of God. It should be the concern of all believers to avoid division and chaos with each other and to accept and embrace each other because that is God's plan.

Romans 15:7-13 emphasizes the intended character of the church: we are all to be one in Jesus Christ, whether we're weak or strong, Jew or Gentile. Paul there says, "Wherefore, receive ye one another, as Christ also received us to the glory of God. Now I say that Jesus Christ was a minister of the circumcision for the truth of God, to confirm the promises made unto the fathers, and that the Gentiles might glorify God for his mercy; as it is written, For this cause I will confess to thee among the nations, and sing unto thy name. And again he saith, Rejoice ye nations, with his people. And again, Praise the Lord, all ye nations; and laud him, all ye peoples. And again, Isaiah saith, There shall be a root of Jesse, and he that shall rise to reign over the nations; in him shall the nations trust. Now the God of hope fill you with all joy and peace in believing, that ye may abound in hope, through the power of the Holy Spirit." That is Paul's final call for unity among weak and strong, and he emphasizes the importance of rejoicing together.

According to His saving plan, God has brought all people together: Jew and Gentile, weak and strong, and made them one in Christ. In this passage Paul no longer exhorts us in a negative manner but calls us to rejoice in what God has done in making us one. The key to overcoming conflict in the church is not only to prohibit negative behavior but also to cultivate a corporate attitude of joy and praise.

When Paul mentions strong believers in Romans 14:1–15:13, he primarily (but not exclusively) has in mind Gentiles—pagans who have no relationship to Old Testament law. When he mentions weak believers, he primarily has in mind Jews, who for the most part continue to hold onto Old Testament ceremony. The strong were right—they did have freedom—and the weak were wrong. But Paul calls for the strong to love the weak until they can understand their freedom.

Lesson

I. THE BASIC INSTRUCTION (v. 7)

"Wherefore, receive ye one another, as Christ also received us to the glory of God."

Since according to verse 6 God wants us to glorify Him with one mind (internally) and one mouth (externally), we have to receive one another. We see the same verb used in Romans 14:1, where Paul makes a similar point: "Him that is weak in the faith, receive." But in Romans 15:7 Paul calls all believers to open their arms and embrace other believers. The strong are to receive the weak, and the weak are to receive the strong. The Jews are to receive the Gentiles, and the Gentiles are to receive the Jews.

103

A. The Intensity of the Command

The Greek word commonly translated "receive" (*lambanō*) is intensified by the addition a strong preposition (*pros*). It means "to receive by pulling someone or something very close to yourself."

1. The illustrations

a) Mark 8:32—"[Jesus] spoke that saying openly. And Peter took [received] him, and began to rebuke him." Peter pulled Jesus aside and rebuked Him about foretelling His death. The primary use of the Greek word here translated "took" is of pulling someone in intimately.

b) Acts 17:5—"The Jews who believed not, moved with envy, took unto them certain vile fellows of the baser sort, and gathered a company, and set all the city in an uproar." The Jews pulled those evil men away from the crowd into a private conversation.

c) Acts 18:24-26—"A certain Jew, named Apollos, born at Alexandria, an eloquent man, and mighty in the scriptures, came to Ephesus. . . . And he began to speak boldly in the synagogue; whom, when Aquila and Priscilla had heard, they took him unto them, and expounded unto him the way of God more perfectly." They pulled Apollos away from ministering to the crowd into private counsel.

d) Acts 27:33-34, 36—Three times in this passage *proslambanō* is used for taking in food.

e) Acts 28:2—Paul and the crew escaped from their shipwreck and landed on the island of Melita (Malta). In verse 2 Luke says, "The barbarous people showed us no little kindness; for they kindled a fire, and received us, every one, because of the present rain, and because of the cold." They showed hospitality to Paul and the men.

f) Philemon 12, 17—Paul told Philemon to receive Onesimus, his servant, when the latter returned (v.

12). In verse 17 he says, "If thou count me, therefore, a partner, receive him as myself."

2. The implications

So in Romans 15:7 Paul is saying to receive one another warmly in love. What a wonderful command! The implications of it are made more wonderful when we look at Matthew 10:40, where Jesus says, "He that receiveth you receiveth me, and he that receiveth me receiveth him that sent me." When you receive another believer, you receive Christ. In receiving Christ, you are receiving the one who sent Him—God the Father. So you are to lovingly receive your brother in Christ, even though he may live a different life-style or may not enjoy his liberty to the same extent as you.

a) For the Gentile

It was hard for a liberated Gentile, who was not confined to Old Testament law, to accept a legalistic Jew. The Gentile tended to look down on such a person and say, "Why can't you accept your freedom?"

b) For the Jew

The weak Jew, bound by ceremonial law, had a difficult time accepting any Gentile, let alone accepting a liberated Gentile. It was hard for him to conceive of God's allowing a brotherhood of Gentiles to be on equal terms with Jews, particularly because the Gentiles had no regard for Old Testament ceremony.

To the Jews, the Gentiles appeared to be guilty of abusive license. To the Gentiles, the Jews appeared to be guilty of a lack of faith. So the potential for conflict was great. Both needed to understand the principle of Romans 15:7: accepting believers as they are. One of the most devastating things that can happen in a church is when people set up criteria for receiving each other. If some don't meet that criteria, then they are shut out from fellowship or made to feel not welcome.

B. The Pattern of the Command

Romans 15:7 says, "Receive ye one another, as Christ also received us." Christ is our pattern. In Matthew 11:29 Jesus says, "Take my yoke upon you, and learn of me." He is telling us not only to learn about His gospel, but also to learn about His character and His approach to life.

1. Christ's merciful standard

Ephesians 4:32–5:2 makes clear that Christ is our model: "Be ye kind one to another, tenderhearted, forgiving one another, even as God, for Christ's sake, hath forgiven you. Be ye, therefore, followers of God, as dear children; and walk in love, as Christ also hath loved us, and hath given himself for us an offering and a sacrifice to God for a sweet-smelling savor." Were you worthy of Christ's receiving you? Did He receive you because you were so wonderful? Did He receive me because I was irresistible? Not at all! In Luke 15:2 the Pharisees and scribes say, "This man receiveth sinners." Christ received us when we hated Him and God, when we were steeped in sin. If He did not refuse to love us; embrace us; forgive us; call us His friends, children, and brothers; to live within us; empower us; and call us to assist Him in the development of His kingdom, should we not receive each other?

2. Christians' merciless standard

When a Christian refuses to receive another Christian into his heart, in effect he is saying, "I know Christ receives the worst of sinners, but I require more. I have a higher standard." Are you more holy than He is? Can He be friends with people not worthy of your friendship? Can He receive people who aren't good enough for you and me? That's a blasphemous thought. For people in the Body of Christ to refuse to open their hearts to one another is to claim a different standard from Christ's.

Now, nothing we do can compare to the sacrifice of Christ and His reception of sinners, but the illustration still stands. As He received those who were unworthy, so we must receive each other. Your failure to open your heart to other believers because you resent something about them is an affront to Christ who received you. If we place restraints on our love for one another, we are violating the principle of Romans 15:7 and the model of redemptive love Himself.

C. The Reason for the Command

1. The purpose

According to Romans 15:7, Christ received us "to the glory of God." That's the reason for our receiving each other. When we receive each other we reflect the love of Christ shed abroad in our hearts. Since that is His expressed will, it brings Him praise. My prayer for the church is that we might have that attitude. I constantly hear of all kinds of squabbles among Christians in church congregations. There will be differences in our understanding of Christian freedom, but that is not a cause for division.

2. The pattern

Matthew 10:24 says, "The disciple is not above his teacher, nor the servant above his lord." If Christ received sinners, then we ought to receive each other.

How does Christ receive sinners? Let me give you four answers.

a) Christ receives sinners with joy

(1) The illustration

Luke 15:1-7 says, "Then drew near unto him all the tax collectors and sinners to hear him. And the Pharisees and scribes murmured, saying, This man receiveth sinners, and eateth with them. And he spoke this parable unto them, saying, What man of you, having an hundred sheep, if he lose one of them, doth not leave the ninety and nine in the wilderness, and go after that which is lost, until he find it? And when he hath found it, he layeth it on his shoulders, rejoicing. And when he cometh home, he calleth together his friends and neighbors, saying unto them, Rejoice with me; for I have found my sheep which was lost. I say unto you that likewise joy shall be in heaven over one sinner that repenteth, more than over ninety and nine righteous persons, who need no repentance."

(2) The principle

Christ receives the sinner gladly, not reluctantly:

(a) Matthew 23:37—"O Jerusalem, Jerusalem, thou that killest the prophets, and stonest them who are sent unto thee, how often would I have gathered thy children together, even as a hen gathereth her chickens under her wings, and ye would not!"

(b) Matthew 11:28—"Come unto me, all ye that labor and are heavy laden, and I will give you rest."

(c) John 7:37—"If any man thirst, let him come unto me, and drink."

(d) John 8:12—"I am the light of the world; he that followeth me shall not walk in darkness."

(e) John 5:40—"Ye will not come to me, that ye might have life."

(f) Luke 23:34—"Father, forgive them; for they know not what they do."

(g) John 6:37—"Him that cometh to me I will in no wise cast out."

(3) The application

We should receive one another with gladness, not with condescension or reluctance. When I was traveling through the South, I heard about a

white pastor who opened his heart to teach the
Bible to a black man. As the pastor began to disciple this man, the people of the church asked him
to stop because he was creating a racial problem.
But the pastor continued. As a result, he was un-
able to buy gas at the local station or groceries in
the local store. His insurance was canceled, and
his children were harassed. Yet the sign outside
the church read, "Come unto me, all ye that labor
and are heavy laden, and I will give you rest."
That situation illustrates how a church can hold
to a biblical theology as an identifying mark of its
fellowship yet in its heart be living in the opposite
realm. We are to receive one another with gladness, not reluctantly or condescendingly.

b) Christ receives sinners despite their sin

People don't have to clean up their lives before Christ
receives them. That's heresy. There is no pre-salva-
tion work any man can do to make himself acceptable
to Christ. The Lord receives sinners despite their sin.
That's the beauty of grace.

(1) The illustrations

(a) Christ's relationship with sinners

Matthew 9:10-13 says, "As Jesus sat eating in
the house, behold, many tax collectors and
sinners came and sat down with him and his
disciples. And when the Pharisees saw it,
they said unto his disciples, Why eateth your
Master with tax collectors and sinners? But
when Jesus heard that, he said unto them,
They that are well need not a physician, but
they that are sick. But go and learn what that
meaneth, I will have mercy, and not sacrifice;
for I am not come to call the righteous, but
sinners to repentance." Christ came for those
who are sinners.

(*b*) Christ's reception of a sinner

> Luke 18:10-14 says, "Two men went up into the temple to pray; the one a Pharisee, and the other a tax collector. The Pharisee stood and prayed thus with himself, God, I thank thee that I am not as other men are, extortioners, unjust, adulterers, or even as this tax collector. I fast twice in the week; I give tithes of all that I possess. And the tax collector, standing afar off, would not lift up so much as his eyes unto heaven, but smote upon his breast, saying, God, be merciful to me a sinner. I tell you, this man went down to his house justified rather than the other."

(2) The principle

> Jesus receives sinners despite their sin, even though they are depraved, despairing of righteousness, and helpless. In Romans 5:8 Paul says, "God commendeth his love toward us in that, while we were yet sinners, Christ died for us." In his own testimony Paul said, "Christ Jesus came into the world to save sinners, of whom I am chief" (1 Tim. 1:15). Christ drew sinners to Himself to change their sins and their imperfections, to make them like Himself.

c) Christ receives sinners without partiality

Acts 10:34 and Romans 2:11 tell us that God is no respecter of persons. It doesn't matter to God whether you're Jew or Gentile, male or female, bond or free. Your background doesn't matter to God.

He calls for the same attitude from us in James 2:1-9: "My brethren, have not the faith of our Lord Jesus Christ, the Lord of glory, with respect of persons. For if there come unto your assembly a man with a gold ring, in fine apparel, and there come in also a poor man in vile raiment, and ye have respect to him that weareth the fine clothing, and say unto him, Sit thou here in a good place; and say to the poor, Stand thou

110

there, or sit here under my footstool, are ye not then partial in yourselves, and are become judges with evil thoughts? Hearken, my beloved brethren, Hath not God chosen the poor of this world to be rich in faith and heirs of the kingdom which he hath promised to them that love him? But ye have despised the poor. Do not rich men oppress you, and draw you before the judgment seats? Do not they blaspheme that worthy name by the which ye are called? If ye fulfill the royal law according to the scripture, Thou shalt love thy neighbor as thyself, ye do well. But if ye have respect of persons, ye commit sin, and are convicted of the law as transgressors."

There is no place for having respect of persons in the church. Christ set the example in John 6:37: "Him that cometh to me I will in no wise cast out."

d) Christ receives sinners to glorify God

God is glorified when sinners are saved. Ephesians 1:4-6 says, "He hath chosen us in him before the foundation of the world, that we should be holy and without blame before him, in love having predestinated us unto the adoption of sons by Jesus Christ to himself, according to the good pleasure of His will, to the praise of the glory of his grace." The reason God saved you was for His own glory—that He might demonstrate His glory to all principalities and powers, to the angelic host, and to all created beings. Ephesians 3:10 says His intent is to show "the principalities and powers in heavenly places . . . the manifold wisdom of God."

Everything ultimately resolves itself in God's glory—His sovereign electing grace, His predestination, His will, His shed blood, and His saving work. Christ receives sinners with joy despite their sin, without partiality, and for God's glory. He's our model.

II. THE BIBLICAL ILLUSTRATIONS (vv. 8-12)

Paul illustrates the fact of unity between Jew and Gentile in Christ by choosing four Old Testament prophecies to verify Gentile salvation. They reveal that the coming Messiah would receive the nations of the world and make them partakers of the covenant of grace. It was Paul's intention to soften Jewish prejudice in the church at Rome, leading Jewish Christians to rejoice over Gentile salvation as the fulfillment of Old Testament prophecy, rather than to create division and dissension over it.

The Jew / Gentile Factor in Romans

The epistle to the Romans is preoccupied with the unity of Jew and Gentile in Christ.

1. Chapter 1—Verse 5 tell us that the gospel comes "for obedience to the faith among all nations." The gospel is for all nations. In verse 13 Paul states he wants to see fruit among the Gentiles. In verse 14 he says, "I am debtor both to the Greeks and to the barbarians; both to the wise and to the unwise." Verse 16 says that the gospel "is the power of God unto salvation to everyone that believeth; to the Jew first, and also to the Greek." The epistle is filled with the theme of Gentile conversion.

2. Chapter 2—In verses 14-15 Paul says, "When the Gentiles, who have not the law, do by nature the things contained in the law, these, having not the law, are a law unto themselves; who show the work of the law written in their hearts." In verse 24 Paul tells the Jews that their conduct causes the name of God to be blasphemed among the Gentiles. God wanted the Jews to evangelize the Gentiles, not to dishonor Him before them.

3. Chapter 3—Verse 19 says that every mouth is stopped and the whole world is guilty before God. Verse 29 points out that God is not only the God of the Jews but also the God of the Gentiles. All men are sinners, and all have the same God to turn to for salvation.

4. Chapter 5—Verse 12 says, "Death passed upon all men, for all have sinned." Verse 15 says, "Not as the offense [that all have sinned], so also is the free gift. For if through the offense of one

many are dead, much more the grace of God, and the gift by grace, which is by one man, Jesus Christ, hath abounded unto many." Then verse 17 says, "If by one man's offense death reigned by one, much more they who receive abundance of grace and of the gift of righteousness shall reign in life by one, Jesus Christ."

5. Chapter 9—In verses 24-25 Paul says, "Even us, whom he hath called, not of the Jews only, but also of the Gentiles? As he saith also in Hosea, I will call them my people, who were not my people; and her beloved, who was not beloved." That refers to the Gentiles whom God has allowed to enter into His New Covenant. Verse 30 says, "The Gentiles, who followed not after righteousness, have attained to righteousness."

6. Chapter 10—In verses 12-13 Paul says, "There is no difference between the Jew and the Greek; for the same Lord over all is rich unto all that call upon him. For whosoever shall call upon the name of the Lord shall be saved."

7. Chapter 11—Verse 11 says, "Through their fall [the fall of the Jews] salvation is come unto the Gentiles." Verse 25 says that the fullness of the Gentiles will come along with the salvation of Israel.

Paul begins Romans by showing that the whole world is in sin. He ends by showing that both the saved Jew and Gentile will be brought together in unity in Christ. Romans is a declaration of God's sovereign act to save both Jew and Gentile.

  A. The Proof of Equal Salvation (vv. 8-9a)

    1. Showing Jews the truth of God (v. 8)

      "Now I say that Jesus Christ was a minister of the circumcision for the truth of God, to confirm the promises of God made unto the fathers.

      a) Jesus fulfilled prophecy

        Jesus was a servant of the circumcision, meaning He came as a Jew to the Jews. As a child He was circumcised and identified physically with the sign of the covenant. Jesus said, "I am not sent but unto the lost sheep of the house of Israel" (Matt. 15:24). He came as a servant to the Jews to confirm the promises God made to the fathers. Who were the fathers? Abraham, Isaac, and Jacob. After giving His covenant to Abraham, God reiterated it to both Isaac and Jacob. He promised that a great deliverer would come. Jesus came to fulfill prophecy.

b) Jesus verified God's truth

The truth of God was at stake. Romans 15:8 says Jesus came "for the truth of God." He came to verify God's Word to the Jewish people. In Matthew 5:17-18 Jesus says, "Think not that I am come to destroy the law, or the prophets; I am not come to destroy, but to fulfill. For verily I say unto you, Till heaven and earth pass, one jot or one tittle shall in no way pass from the law, till all be fulfilled." Christ fulfilled the law by upholding its sacredness, re-establishing its truth, and keeping it perfectly. He came to confirm God's covenant, and He did so with His own blood.

(1) The testimony of Mary

When Mary learned about the child she was carrying she proclaimed, "My soul doth magnify the Lord" (Luke 1:46). Then she concluded, "As he spoke to our fathers, to Abraham, and to his seed forever" (Luke 1:55). She realized God was doing what He told Abraham He would do.

(2) The testimony of Zacharias

When Zacharias was filled with the Holy Spirit after the birth of his own child, John the Baptist, he said, "Blessed be the Lord God of Israel; for he hath visited and redeemed his people, and hath raised up an horn of salvation for us in the house of his servant, David; as he spoke by the mouth of his holy prophets" (Luke 1:68-70).

2. Showing Gentiles the mercy of God (v. 9*a*)

"That the Gentiles might glorify God for his mercy."

Certainly the Jews are thankful for God's mercy, and the Gentiles are thankful for His truth, but Paul's emphasis is that Christ came to show the Jews the truth of God and the Gentiles the mercy of God. The saved Jew will primarily praise God for His truth—that He made a promise and kept it. The saved Gentile will primarily praise God for His mercy—that He extended His grace to a people outside the Covenant.

When the saved Jew and saved Gentile are blended together, they with one mind and one voice will glorify God. God's truthfulness is important to Israel. God's mercy is important to the Gentiles. But both will glorify God and rejoice that they have been included in the plan of God. In Isaiah 45:22 God says, "Look unto me, and be saved, all the ends of the earth." Isaiah 52:10 says, "All the ends of the earth shall see the salvation of our God."

B. The Promise of Equal Salvation (vv. 9*b*-12)

To show the promise of salvation for the Gentiles, Paul quotes four Old Testament passages.

1. Psalm 18:49 (v. 9*b*)

"As it is written, For this cause I will confess to thee among the nations, and sing unto thy name."

The Greek word translated "confess" means to acknowledge God. In this verse the psalmist says he will acknowledge God in the middle of the nations. The psalmist sings praise to God among the nations, which alludes to Gentile salvation.

2. Deuteronomy 32:43 (v. 10)

"And again, he saith, Rejoice ye nations, with his people."

Here Gentiles are rejoicing along with the Jews.

115

3. Psalm 117:1 (v. 11)

"And again, Praise the Lord, all ye nations; and laud him, all ye peoples."

In this verse we see all nations and all people praising God.

4. Isaiah 11:1, 10 (v. 12)

"And again, Isaiah saith, There shall be a root of Jesse, and he that shall rise to reign over the nations; in him shall the nations trust."

Jesse was the father of David. It was from the Davidic line that the Messiah came. He will one day rise out of His humiliation as the suffering Savior to reign over the nations. He will rule the world. He will reign not just with a rod of iron, but with the trust of the nations. That the nations will hope in the Messiah is a promise of Gentile salvation.

The Old Testament said the Gentiles would be saved and would praise and rejoice with Israel. All are loved by God. The Gentiles can't hold a grudge against the Jews because salvation came to them through the Jews. The Jews can't hold a grudge against the Gentiles because their primary purpose for existence was to reach the Gentiles.

III. THE BENEDICTORY INTERCESSION (v. 13)

"Now the God of hope fill you with all joy and peace in believing, that ye may abound in hope, through the power of the Holy Spirit."

That is the summation of the epistle of Romans. Paul is praying that God, who is the source of eternal hope, life, and salvation, will overflow the believer with all those things. It is Paul's prayer that all believers be spiritually satisfied. He has described the practical outworking of salvation in Romans 12:1–15:13, saying we're to exercise our spiritual gifts, show love to everyone, and be obedient to the government. His concluding point is that we are to be united as brothers and sisters in Christ. Only then will we be fully satisfied in Christ.

Focusing on the Facts

1. What is another way of overcoming conflict besides prohibiting negative behavior (see p. 103)?
2. What does the word *receive* mean as used by Paul in Romans 15:7 (see p. 104)?
3. According to Matthew 10:40, what happens when we receive another believer (see p. 105)?
4. Explain why it was not easy for Gentiles or Jews to receive one another (see p. 105).
5. According to Ephesians 4:32–5:2, what model should we follow (see p. 106)?
6. What is a Christian essentially doing when he refuses to receive another Christian (see p. 106)?
7. According to Romans 15:7, why did Christ receive us? Why should we receive other believers (see p. 107)?
8. Name the four ways Christ received sinners. Explain each (see pp. 107-11).
9. What is Paul's intention in quoting four Old Testament passages in Romans 12:9-12 (see p. 112)?
10. Explain how Romans describes the equality of Jews and Gentiles in the plan of God (see pp. 112-13).
11. Why did Christ come to the Jews as a Jew (see pp. 113-14)?
12. What did Jesus verify when He came (see p. 114)?
13. For what does the saved Gentile praise God (see p. 115)?
14. Why shouldn't Jews or Gentiles hold grudges against one another (see p. 116)?

Pondering the Principles

1. What is your standard for receiving your fellow believers in Christ? Is it the same as Christ's, or have you set up your own? Are there some Christians in your fellowship whom you have intentionally ignored and not received? If so, you need to swallow your pride and go to them as soon as possible. Take them aside and show them you are willing to receive them and fellowship with them. Continue to watch over your relationships with your fellow Christians. Make sure you don't set up a standard that is different from Christ's.

2. Do you receive other believers gladly or reluctantly? Do you receive other believers impartially, treating all with the same respect? You will know some believers better than others, but that doesn't mean you shouldn't treat those you don't know well with any less respect than your closest friend. Do you receive others despite their sins, both past and present, even when it is some sin that is especially repulsive to you? Finally, what is your motive in receiving others? You should desire to receive others to glorify God. If you are lacking in any of those areas, make the commitment today to receive your fellow brothers and sisters in Christ as Jesus Himself has.

3. Read the parable in Luke 18:9-14. To whom did the Pharisee pray? What was his attitude? To whom did the tax collector pray? What was his attitude? What is your attitude when you pray? Does it resemble more the attitude of the Pharisee or that of the tax collector? Whenever you pray from now on, check out two things: To whom are you praying? What is your attitude? Remember, God will hear only the prayer of one who displays the attitude of the tax collector.

Scripture Index

Topical Index

opinion of weak believers, 15
pleasing weak believers, 88-98
receiving weak believers, 22-25, 29-42, 103-11
removing stumbling blocks before weak believers, 14-18, 28-29, 52-54, 56-60, 75-77
temptation of, 13-14, 32-33
See also Liberty in Christ, Maturity, Weak believers
Stumbling blocks. *See* Strong believers
Sunday. *See* Sabbath

Television
addiction to, 49
differing views on watching, 46
neutrality of, 77
self-retardation and, 50-51

Ten Commandments, necessity of obeying, 14
Trials. *See* Endurance
TV. *See* Television

Unity. *See* Church, unity in

Vegetarianism. *See* Food

Weak believers
definition of, 13, 103
destruction of, 31
fear of, 33
legalism of, 18, 32-33
motives of, 35-36
temptation of, 14, 32
view of strong believers, 15
See also Amish, Conscience, Strong Believers
Whites, prejudice of. *See* Prejudice
Witnessing. *See* Evangelism

Moody Press, a ministry of the Moody Bible Institute, is designed for education, evangelization, and edification. If we may assist you in knowing more about Christ and the Christian life, please write us without obligation: Moody Press, c/o MLM, Chicago, Illinois 60610.